The Best Defense

The Best Defense

JOEL MOLDOVSKY

AND

ROSE DeWOLF

MACMILLAN PUBLISHING CO., INC.

NEW YORK

The authors dedicate this book
to Rose's husband,
BERNARD INGSTER
and to Joel's wife,
DORIS MOLDOVSKY

Macmillan Publishing Co., Inc.
866 Third Avenue, New York, N.Y. 10022
Collier-Macmillan Canada Ltd.

Library of Congress Cataloging in Publication Data

Moldovsky, Joel.
   The best defense.

   1. Moldovsky, Joel. 2. Lawyers—Philadelphia—
Correspondence, reminiscences, etc. 3. Philadelphia—
Biography. I. DeWolf, Rose, joint author. II. Title.
KF373.M54D4   345'.73'00924 [B]   75-1154
ISBN 0-02-585590-5

FIRST PRINTING 1975
Printed in the United States of America

Contents

Preface

To be able to pick and choose among innocent clients or very rich clients or very dramatic clients or very idealistic and noble clients is the privilege and practice of very few defense attorneys in this country.

The average big-city criminal lawyer represents the average criminal. He or she represents muggers, murderers, rapists, arsonists, burglars, prostitutes, pimps, and pushers. He represents whoever comes into his office with a fee and he doesn't ask their politics.

The criminal lawyer (despite the publicity given the breed) actually is one of the law's smallest minorities. Most lawyers who are frank consider criminal business a seedy practice—a matter of dealing with people whom they wouldn't ask to lunch. There are many attorneys willing to take an occasional criminal case, but very few willing to take *only* criminal cases. For example, there are six thousand practicing lawyers in the city of Philadelphia. Only one hundred and twenty of these are full-time criminal lawyers. Some one hundred (and that number is really too small to do a decent job) work for the Public Defender's Office, which represents most of the poor who are arrested on criminal charges. Only twenty work privately, successfully, and exclusively at criminal law.

One of these is Joel Moldovsky, who would never want to do anything else. He claims that with criminal cases, as with fingerprints, no two are alike.

Moldovsky has seen the criminal-justice system from two points of view. At thirty-four, he's been both an assistant district attorney and a defense attorney. He has done both with such success that one might say "justice" in Philadelphia has sometimes depended on which side had Moldovsky at the moment (which doesn't necessarily say a lot for justice).

Moldovsky is popular with Philadelphia's courtroom regulars because he is a dramatic performer. The regulars —those retired gentlemen and housewives who enliven their leisure hours by coming to court to watch the proceedings—always know which prosecutors or defense lawyers are likely to give them the best show.

But basically, Moldovsky is a good big-city criminal lawyer who cheerfully admits to working just as hard for the guilty as the innocent and to not always knowing whether a given client is really one or the other.

A criminal-law practice means paying as much attention to pretrial maneuvers as to the trial itself. Some cases are "won" or "lost" before a judge ever sits down on a bench. It involves strategy, tactics, and *chutzpah*.

I suggested to Moldovsky that he discuss all of the above in a book, and he agreed.

One reason he agreed is that he gets annoyed at the phony image of criminal lawyers presented on TV. He says that when he watches Owen Marshall, for example, spend long hours socializing with his clients, concentrating on only one case at a time, representing *only* innocent clients, and never, never mentioning a fee, he wants to chew the rug.

Most people never come in contact with a criminal lawyer—not professionally, anyway. But then most people never get inside a courtroom—not as defendant, witness, or juror.

There are more people who are sure our criminal-justice system "doesn't work" than are sure *how* it works. A lot of people, for example, think a trial by jury is a very common thing. It isn't. It's actually rather rare. Out of some fifteen thousand criminal trials held in Philadelphia last year, only two hundred were before juries.

Not too long ago someone suggested that I write a story about "the way judges can be bought."

"Just like that?" I said. "Do you have a particular judge in mind? What makes you think he's on the take?"

"It was obvious," this person said. "The judge let a murderer go scot-free. What happened was that a friend of mine was struck by a hit-and-run driver. He dragged her body two miles, then dumped her, leaving her to die. The driver was caught by the police and charged with murder. But when the man was brought to court, zap—he was acquitted. I wasn't at the hearing, but it had to be a payoff. There is no other explanation."

"I can think of at least a half-dozen other explanations right off—all of which are as likely, if not even more likely than a payoff," I said. Some of my other explanations would go like this:

—The man brought before the judge didn't do it. It turns out that, upon further investigation, the police learn the man's car was stolen that night. The actual culprit was a car thief whose identity is still unknown. The district attorney asks the judge to dismiss charges.

—The man brought before the judge convinces the judge that he was not aware he had struck a human being. He tells the judge he thought he'd hit a small animal. He felt bad about this, but it was late at night on a lonely road and he was afraid to get out of his car to check. The judge has reasonable doubt of the man's guilt.

—The district attorney has decided not to push this case at all. He decides it wasn't an intentional murder and he has a huge backlog of intentional murders to worry about. Since in a case like this the victim's family can sue the driver for civil damages in a wrongful death action, the DA decides not to spend the taxpayer's money pursuing a criminal charge.

—The driver, when questioned by police, admitted hitting the woman with his car and even signed a statement. But it develops that the police did not warn him of his rights before taking the statement or he was detained for ten hours before the statement was taken. Therefore, the judge, by law, must suppress the statement—not allow it to be used as evidence. There is no other evidence and the judge has no choice but to acquit.

—The judge has a personal idiosyncrasy that makes him tend to favor motorists over pedestrians. The defense attorney knows that this judge rants and raves about the way pedestrians walk on roads and cross against lights and otherwise endanger themselves. So the defense attorney has maneuvered to get this case before this judge.

—Maybe the defendant is the judge's nephew.

—Maybe racial prejudice is involved.

Maybe a lot of things. Nothing about our system of justice is cut and dried. There is never anything "obvious" about what happens or why it happens. Sometimes the least obvious thing in a courtroom is the existence of guilt or innocence.

I've seen defendants I believed were innocent plead guilty in return for a guaranteed suspended sentence because they didn't want to spend the kind of money a defense would have cost them.

I've seen defendants I was sure were guilty walk away smiling because witnesses failed to show up. I've seen witnesses show up ten times—missing a day's pay each time to do so—only to find the case had been postponed.

In one case I don't think I'll ever forget, the victim went to jail but the villain did not. The victim was a decent, law-abiding woman who was viciously attacked by a neighborhood crazy one night as she was walking on the street. He actually cut her throat and she was on the operating table for four hours. She was in critical condition for days and was out of work for weeks.

Her attacker, whom she'd recognized, was duly arrested and released in five-hundred-dollars' bail for later appearance in court. The accused was granted postponements every time he showed up in court. He had legitimate reasons—at least they seemed so to the court. But the victim got tired of continually showing up and going home again. So when the case was set for trial once again, five years after the original attack had happened, the discouraged victim decided it wasn't worth the bother, and she didn't show up in court.

Neither did the accused.

The judge issued bench warrants for *both* of them. The

police found the victim, who wasn't hiding, but not the accused, who apparently was. And so the *victim* landed in jail for contempt of court. She was photographed, fingerprinted, handcuffed, and taken away to jail, where she stayed for two days.

The man who cut her throat never spent five minutes in jail.

You can expect to see and hear almost anything in criminal court. When you read what Joel has to say about his career so far, you'll know why.

In some of the stories that follow, names and small nonmaterial details or descriptions have been changed to protect the innocent, and the guilty too. However, some cases have had so much publicity, it seems pointless to try to disguise them.

In some cases where Moldovsky describes what a client has said to him, he is not, I hasten to point out, violating the confidentiality of the lawyer-client relationship. In these specifically selected cases, the client's story became a matter of public record either in court or in newspaper stories. Except for one gentleman we have dubbed Charlie Farnsworth, all names of lawyers and judges used here are real ones. We have also used real names (except for a few as noted) in chapters 2, 3, 7, 9, 10, and 16. In Chapter 15, the names in the Willie Sutton story are real, but the names in the Harry Bartlett story are not. Otherwise all other names in the book have been changed.

On the subject of the public record, Joel was loathe to discuss the case of Myers Douglas Thomas (Chapter 7) because the case is still pending in the courts. However, this book, although written in the first person, is, in fact, a collaboration between an attorney and a journalist. And in the matter of Myers Douglas Thomas, the journalist half (who was able to get the material from court records and newspapers) managed to overrule the attorney half and include the story.

One last comment: This book is not about justice as it should be, but as it is.

R. DEW.

Philadelphia, September 1974

1

All My Clients
Are Innocent

I like to say that all my clients are innocent. And as a matter of fact, that's true according to the Constitution of the United States—until they are proven guilty.

I know that a lot of people think that although I may not know in advance which of my clients *will be proven* guilty, I always know in advance which ones *should be.* But that's not the way it is.

Sometimes all I know when a client tells me he didn't do it is that either he didn't do it or he lies well.

When Ramon Rivera, a young Puerto Rican, asked me to represent him, he cried. Crying doesn't necessarily mean a man is innocent, but Rivera was really hysterical, and, I don't know why, but I was convinced this man wasn't just putting on an act. He had been referred to me by an assistant district attorney who saw him at his preliminary hearing and I guess the ADA was somehow impressed by him too.

The charge against Rivera was atrocious assault. The

police said he had walked up to a car waiting for a light, reached inside with a razor blade, and for no apparent reason slashed the driver's face.

The district attorney was ready for trial, with the driver, the passenger in the car, and the arresting officer all ready to positively identify my client, even though he hadn't been caught in the act but was arrested later on the street.

Ramon claimed that on that particular night he left work (he was a grocery store clerk), went to a bar with some friends, had a couple of drinks, and then walked toward a local restaurant. Two policemen picked him up, drove him to a hospital, and showed him to a man with a cut face, who said, "That's him."

The policemen had arrested my client because he fit the description given by the complainant of the man who had cut him: blue jacket, brown work pants. On top of that, the police found a razor-type cutter in Rivera's pocket. Rivera claimed that he had the cutter because he used it to open boxes at the grocery store.

I went into court to suppress the identification. I claimed there was an illegal confrontation. That was nothing novel—it's a standard defense approach. I said it would have been fair to have five or six young men of Puerto Rican background in a lineup to see if the driver could pick out the man he claimed attacked him. But if you show him just one Puerto Rican and he identifies that man, he's going to stick to that identification. Maybe he just doesn't like Puerto Rican people and doesn't care which Puerto Rican pays the penalty as long as one does.

Maybe I believed Rivera, but the fact was that he didn't have an alibi. He didn't have any defense except his denial and my ability to suppress or shake those positive identifications.

I have a theory about courtroom identifications. If you ask a witness to point out the assailant, he'll automatically point to the person sitting next to the defense lawyer. Witnesses just assume that's the defendant and the defendant is guilty.

So with the permission of the judge, I sat Rivera's brother Fidel next to me at the defense table and left Ramon outside the courtroom with a guard. This brother looked nothing like Ramon. Ramon was twenty-two, Fidel was thirty-four. Fidel was a head taller, he wore glasses, he had long sideburns. They didn't even look like brothers.

Then I casually asked the DA's witnesses if they saw the guilty man in the courtroom, and they said yes and pointed to Fidel. That was the end of the DA's case; it never went to a jury. The judge threw it out right there.

Any lawyer reading this won't believe I got the judge's permission for this caper. I have to admit that under ordinary circumstances an attorney can be held in contempt of court for having the wrong man sitting in the defendant's chair. Before a trial starts, the defendant must stand, identify himself, be sworn, and answer certain questions.

A lawyer cannot let the wrong man lie under oath about who he is. A lawyer is an officer of the court and cannot mislead the court. And yet, there are so many cases of mistaken identity that you would think the courts would make some provision for this kind of defense. An assistant district attorney in New York even went to jail for a while because he was identified as a rapist. And he stayed in jail until police caught a rapist who looked remarkably like him.

Juries, I've found, are very impressed by courtroom identifications. When somebody sits in the witness box, looks at your client, and says, "Yes, that's the man. He did it," that's impressive. You can sometimes get around everything else—a confession was forced, a fingerprint was smudged—but when that identification is made, there goes the jury. The weakest kind of evidence then can make the strongest impression.

The way I convinced the judge to make an exception in the Rivera case was to arrange for the identification before anyone was sworn. I walked into the courtroom with Fidel, the brother. I sat him down at the table and walked over to the DA.

"Look," I said, "in the interest of saving time, I'd like to have my client's trial immediately after the suppression hearing. If the judge suppresses the identification as unfair, fine, but if not, we could go right on with the trial and all the identification testimony would then not have to be repeated."

All the time I'm talking, I'm looking at the brother. "Are your witnesses really sure?" I asked the DA. His witnesses were right there and they chimed in to say that of course they were sure. They looked right at Fidel. "No doubt about it, that's the man."

And so even before the first proceeding—the suppression hearing—got underway, I was able to tell the judge at the sidebar that the DA's witnesses had identified the wrong man.

"WHAAAAT?" yelps the DA. "Where is the defendant?"

"He had to go to the bathroom," I said.

The judge then decided to see for himself. The wit-

nesses hadn't been able to hear what I'd told the judge.
So he asked each one in turn to point out the assailant
and of course they pointed to Fidel. Then I put Fidel on
the stand and he testified that he'd never been arrested.

End of case.

The point is that I couldn't actually prove that my
client was innocent. All I could prove, or needed to prove
to the court, to myself, to anyone, was that the other side
couldn't prove him guilty.

One time I defended a friend of mine who had been
arrested for sodomy and corrupting the morals of a minor.
When his wife called me, she was so embarrassed she
didn't know how to tell me what the problem was.

Now this was a guy I knew; not closely, but my wife
and I had been to his house and he and his wife to mine.
He didn't seem the type, but then I've been around
enough types to know that you never know who is.

This kind of charge is not a nice one to hang over anybody's head, but it was particularly appalling for my
friend, Terry Buck, because Terry was employed as a
youth worker at a center for delinquent boys. He had
been arrested in Fairmount Park with a ten-year-old boy
in his car.

Naturally there were two versions to the story.

Terry and his wife were at home when this little boy,
a neighbor, stopped by to collect for UNICEF. Mrs.
Buck gave the boy a contribution. Then Terry said he
was going to go around the neighborhood, too, to canvass
for political contributions for a man then running for
mayor. He suggested that he and the youngster go together. And they set off.

According to Terry, what happened next is that he saw

5

the little boy taking money from the UNICEF container and putting it in his own pocket. "Are you keeping that money?" he said. The boy sheepishly admitted he was.

"I think you and I should take a little drive," Terry said. He put the little boy in his Volkswagen and drove to the park. There he stopped the car, leaned back in the seat, put his feet up on the dashboard, and in friendly fashion gave the boy a Dutch-uncle lecture about honesty.

Would this be reasonable behavior from somebody who every working day of his life deals with delinquent kids? Sure.

However, the ten-year-old's version of the story, as related in court, went this way: "I asked him, Mr. Buck, to take me for a ride and he took me to the park and he parked his car and he pulled down his pants and he asked me to suck his penis and I did and then the sergeant came."

There was no doubt that a sergeant of the park police did appear on the scene. The sergeant said he saw a little head pop up in this parked car and what looked like an older man arranging his pants. So he arrested Terry on the spot. Terry said all the park policeman had seen was him taking his feet off the dash and the little boy sitting up straight, prepared to now drive home.

The first thing I did in Terry Buck's case was to go see his boss.

And just as Terry had feared, the boss said that no matter what the outcome of the trial, Terry was out of a job. "I've got great faith in Terry," the man said. "But remember, this place deals with delinquents. Once word of this kind of thing gets around, the boys will accuse Terry of sodomy every time they get angry at him. For his sake as well as for ours, he'd better look elsewhere."

I cross-examined this youngster at the trial. He was crying the whole time he was on the witness stand. It was no pleasure.

"Didn't you take the money from the can?"

"No."

"Did you say, 'I'm going to give this much to the teacher?' "

"No, I didn't say that."

"What did you say about it?"

"I didn't say nothing."

I attacked the question from every direction and got nowhere. And then I asked, "Are you afraid today that some charges will be placed against you for saying you were taking money from UNICEF?"

The kid nodded his head . . . yes.

So what does that mean? It could mean that the kid was not used to testifying in court and in the end I had merely confused him. Or it could mean that I had out-foxed a little kid who had only said something "dirty" about Terry because he was afraid Terry would turn him in as a thief.

It was up to the judge to decide who was telling the truth. I had lined up character witnesses for Terry. And yet the kid had character witnesses too, in the sense that he came from a very nice family. He was known as a good kid . . . and he looked like one.

It may well be that what finally tipped the scales in the Terry Buck case had nothing to do with either Terry or the ten-year-old.

When I was detailing for the judge my client's exemplary life, I mentioned he'd spent four years in the Navy. The assistant DA made a crack about that. He objected to my mentioning the military, said it wasn't relevant, and added, "You know what they say about Navy men anyway." Ha-ha. It turned out the judge was an old Navy man. He ordered both of us into his chambers and demanded an apology from the assistant DA. He then went back to the bench and acquitted my client.

Actually, I think the judge probably felt there just wasn't a strong enough case to convict anyway—but that crack sure didn't hurt.

What *really* happened out in the park? I wasn't there.

Just as I wasn't around the day a policeman grabbed Donald Washington and charged him with pushing drugs. Don Washington had never had any previous brush with the law and he was not a dope addict. This would actually be held against him if he were convicted as a pusher. Judges tend to be more lenient with someone who sells scag only because he is desperate to make enough money to finance his own supply. But someone who sells just to make money, period, is likely to receive a dose of justice he won't soon forget.

What had happened was that a captain's man—that's a police officer who represents the precinct captain on special complaints—had just come from a meeting with local ministers concerned about neighborhood drug problems. He was in a patrol car and stopped for a light.

He said he looked around and saw my client, Don Washington, hand a packet of heroin—a glassine bag—to a codefendant named Harold Prentice and saw Prentice hand money back to Washington. The officer jumped out of his car, ran up to the men, made Prentice drop his pants and his underpants right there on the street—onlookers notwithstanding—and a bag of heroin fell out.

It may seem rotten to make a man strip on the street, but the police know that if a drug suspect disposes of the heroin while you are transferring him to a car or a building, he has also disposed of your case. At any rate, there was evidence against Prentice, and Prentice had a long record of being a junkie.

The evidence was not clear in Washington's case. He claimed he'd been in a bar at that corner—he'd been laid off his job as a truckdriver and had time to kill—and had just come out the front door when the police officer rushed up and grabbed him. He said the police officer may have seen something but not him.

It seemed to me that the entire case rested on whether the officer could actually see a glassine bag being transferred. There was no doubt that the bag existed, but then Prentice might have been carrying it around or maybe he had just gotten it from somebody else.

At first the officer said he'd only been two feet away. But we established in court that he couldn't have been. His car was at least one traffic lane away—that's ten feet —plus the width of the sidewalk.

I asked the judge if we might perform a demonstration in the court. He agreed.

In the courtroom that day, as usual, there were a lot of police officers waiting to testify as witnesses in cases that would come up later.

"Can I have a volunteer from the audience?" I said. A policeman volunteered. You couldn't accuse me of selecting someone who would be biased for my client.

I had obtained two little bags of the type you'd keep coins in. That's what heroin is sold in. They were called nickel bags then and, inflation being what it is, they are called dime bags now. They are about an inch square. I put white powdered sugar in the bags to represent the heroin.

I proposed to transfer these bags to my policeman volunteer just as the arresting officer claimed my client had transferred a bag to the junkie, at the same distance from the witness stand that the officer would have been from those he arrested. The captain's man gave us directions on how to stand—which hand to use and the like.

I passed a bag. "What did you see?"

"I saw you pass a glassine bag."

I passed a second bag. "What did you see?"

"I saw you pass a glassine bag."

I passed a third object to the policeman. "What did you see?"

"I saw you pass a glassine bag."

"No, you didn't," I said. "Officer, would you show the court what you have in your hand?"

The officer opened his palm and there lay a nice, shiny silver gum wrapper. Silver gum wrappers do not look like white nickel bags. The witness simply made an assumption about what I was handing over. If he'd actually seen it, he'd have seen it was silver.

End of that case. The judge directed a verdict of not guilty.

The strategy I used in defending Donald Washington—a strategy that assumed his innocence—was based simply on his insistence that he was innocent.

I've already admitted I know that clients lie to me . . . I just don't always know which ones are the liars. Take Peter Waring. I believed him.

It was a cold morning in January and a Norman Lombardi, the owner of a discount store in a neighborhood shopping center, had gone to his bank to obtain some change. As he was returning to his store with a coin bag filled with $17 in nickels, dimes, and pennies, he was set upon by a black man wearing a black Russian hat, a black coat, and carrying a gun.

The robber asked Lombardi to hand over the coin bag and he did. Mr. Lombardi later admitted he did not study the robber's face—he was too busy staring at the business end of that gun. However, he was able to say that when the robber fled, he jumped into a car waiting about thirty feet away, in which a second black man was at the wheel. The car made a U turn and sped off. Mr. Lombardi obtained the license-plate number and called the police.

Within fifteen minutes, the police were back to Mr. Lombardi with Peter Waring, Bill Riggins, and a coin bag containing $17. Lombardi told the police he really couldn't identify the robber, but if he had to pick between the two, he'd pick Riggins. Riggins was wearing a black Russian hat and black coat. Yet Riggins, when arrested, had been driving. Waring was the passenger.

Riggins pleaded guilty and was sentenced to four years' probation on the condition that he testify against Waring. A lot of consideration was given Riggins because he had no prior record. He was a bus driver who had a four-year-old daughter with a malignant, inoperable brain tumor. He was desperate from the hospital bills, doctor bills, and mortgage payments piling up. The little girl died within a couple months of the holdup.

Riggins told police that he knew Waring but had not seen him for three years. The morning of the holdup Riggins took his gun from his home, not to commit a robbery but merely because his wife had been so distraught about their daughter, he feared leaving her alone with a gun in the house. He had gotten the gun some years before when he'd worked as a security guard. He just happened to bump into Waring that day at the shopping center. Riggins said he'd gone there to take some clothes to the cleaners.

He told Waring about all his troubles and Waring said, "Give me that gun and I can help you get some money." Waring got out of the car. Riggins went to the cleaners, then got back into the car. Waring came running up, jumped in, said, "Let's go. I got it. I did it." Riggins, panic-stricken, drove away. After they were arrested, said Riggins, Waring told him to keep quiet; he, Waring, would make sure Riggins was not convicted.

Meanwhile, released on bail, Waring skipped to Baltimore and stayed there a year. He said he'd left because he was afraid—he had no way to prove his story. He said Riggins had lied about him to get a light sentence. The Baltimore police located Waring and returned him to Philadelphia.

Waring's version was very believable. He said he had nothing at all to do with the holdup. He'd been out apartment-hunting, had seen his old acquaintance Riggins when Riggins' car stopped at a light. Riggins offered to drive him to the next address on his list. The next thing Waring knew, the police had arrested both of them. Waring's theory was that Riggins had committed the holdup, then dropped off whoever was driving the car at the time, took over the wheel, and then met up with Waring.

Well, after all, it was Riggins who had the motive for robbery, not Waring. It was Riggins' gun. It was Riggins who was wearing the Russian hat and the black coat when arrested. I tried the hat on Riggins in court and it was a perfect fit. Mr. Lombardi testified that he didn't recognize Waring at all, repeating that if he had to pick between the two, he'd pick Riggins. It all seemed to fit. I was on my way for an acquittal for sure.

Until, while my client is still on the witness stand, the district attorney whips out a letter. This letter is addressed to William Riggins and the return address shows the sender to be "Bobby Warner."

When Waring was in Baltimore he had used the name "Bobby Warner" as an alias. I had a certain sinking feeling.

"Is this your handwriting, Mr. Waring?" asks the DA.

"Yes, it is," says my client.

"Permit me, then, to read this letter from Bobby Warner to William Riggins." He is permitted.

"'Greetings Billy,'" he reads. "'I am sure you know why I am here in Baltimore, so I won't have to go into that.'

"'I could have been back there but I thought a delay in our trial would help to weaken the prosecution case and even better influence Mr. Lombardi into not prosecuting because it is entirely too time consuming.'"

He went on to say, "'We can beat this case but we have to work together. If you cooperate with me, I'm going to get you exonerated.'"

To make a long letter short, my client corroborated Riggins' version of the event.

Goodbye acquittal.

I must say that Pete Waring wrote me a very nice letter about the way I'd handled his case. He also wrote me a very nice letter when he read in the newspaper that I was working on this book. I just wish Mr. Waring had told me in advance how much he liked to write letters.

You may wonder whether I ever have a client who claims to be innocent and who I later show *was* innocent —not just that there is reasonable doubt of his guilt, but that there is positive proof he could not possibly have committed the crime.

Many times.

One such client was Walt Hendricks, a thirty-eight-year-old postman, family man, veteran, decent, upstanding citizen.

He was charged with stealing from the United States mails: larceny of mail, receiving stolen goods, conspiracy. Those were just the local charges. At the time he asked me to represent him, the federal charges hadn't been pressed yet.

It seems that welfare checks had been disappearing from the post office. Most of these checks were sent to women, and they were cashed by women with forged signatures. The police said that the proceeds from these checks were considerable and were being used to finance large drug buys.

It was a tough rap . . . stealing from the mail, taking bread out of the mouths of the poor, pushing heroin—a guy could go away forever.

In the course of their investigation, the police had picked up a man named Ron Stevens, who was known to make drug buys, and a woman named Merrilee Johnson, who was known to cash forged checks. The woman, who was an addict, got a few dollars for her role. She told the police that she was given those checks by Stevens, who had gotten them from a postman named Walt Hendricks.

It seemed to check out. Stevens and Hendricks lived in the same neighborhood and knew each other.

The police detectives were really interested in nailing Stevens—he was the one suspected of actually dealing in drugs. They were willing to ask the DA to make a deal if Postman Hendricks turned state's evidence and testified against Stevens. Meanwhile, Stevens and Mrs. Johnson are offering to make a deal for light sentences by offering to testify against this terrible renegade postman, Hendricks.

Hendricks insisted over and over that he was innocent. He couldn't testify against anybody—he wasn't in it at all.

"Can we prove it?" I asked Hendricks. "What day did those three checks given to Merrilee Johnson arrive at the post office? Are you sure you were working that day? Can you check that out?"

Damned if it doesn't turn out that he wasn't working that day. In fact, he wasn't even working that week. He was in the hospital—verifiably, indisputably in the hospital! What's more, he had turned in his post-office keys before going off sick. It turned out that Hendricks had no access to those checks and no opportunity to steal them.

I don't have to point out what a long shot this was, what difficulty Hendricks would have had in establishing his innocence if he had gone to work that day as he did every other day.

Hendricks was working as a detective on his own case; it was his own neck he was saving and he did a very diligent job. He learned that Tom Harmon, the postman whose route was adjacent to his, was actually the most likely suspect.

We figured that when Stevens was stopped by the police and asked to name his check supplier, he just popped off Hendricks' name. He knew Hendricks, he knew Hendricks worked in the post office, and he knew that while the police were busy arresting Hendricks, Harmon would be free to continue to filch checks for Mrs. Johnson to cash, for Stevens to buy dope with. How convenient.

The police might have discovered this on their own, but they thought they had a tight case against Hendricks. They had, after all, two witnesses willing to testify against him as a coconspirator.

Hendricks told me that he had learned enough so that he could take a postal inspector to persons who could testify that Harmon had asked them to cash checks. I took this information to a police detective I'd known while a DA. He was great.

He brought Merrilee Johnson back for questioning and showed her Harmon's picture. He told her he knew Hendricks could not have done it. He told her he knew she was lying. And after a while she admitted it. She said she'd lied because Stevens told her to.

I went to Stevens and suggested he'd better change his story too. He did.

So Walt Hendricks was exonerated—all charges dropped. The case never came to trial. Everybody agreed that they had gone after the wrong man—except the Post Office Department, which didn't want to give him his job back. The fact that Hendricks knew Stevens was sufficient for the Postal Service; they didn't want him. Guilt by association was good enough for them. So my real effort on behalf of Walt Hendricks was not in proving his innocence but in winning his job back. I got together affidavits from the police detectives involved and from the court. It really took some doing, but he was finally reinstated with back pay.

Harmon eventually pleaded guilty to taking the checks.

And meanwhile, I got a brand new client in Stevens. With Stevens I had no illusions about innocence at all. His was the usual defense of trying to wheel and deal for a lower sentence, not an acquittal.

Once Hendricks was out of the picture entirely, I had no conflict of interest in representing Stevens. Stevens was actually the better client: I probably will never get another dollar out of an honest fellow like Walt Hendricks, but Ron Stevens is a defense attorney's bread and butter. His friends tend to need a lawyer—a dope thing here, an assault and battery there. I do have completely innocent clients, but if I restricted my law practice to only innocents, I'd starve to death.

I was able to obtain consideration for Stevens by offering to have him testify against Harmon. Although it was originally Stevens that the DA wanted most, he agreed to a deal to get Harmon, too.

It is cases like that of Walt Hendricks that drive home the lesson that an innocent man can be wrongly accused. Of course, I believe every person—innocent or guilty—deserves the best defense he or she can get. But I will admit I get a certain satisfaction if I can help a truly innocent client prove his case.

2

The Last Resort

A trial by jury is a roll of the dice that you resort to only when the game can't be played any other way.

Every man accused of a serious crime is entitled to be tried by a jury of his peers. Trial by jury is a citizen's guarantee against arbitrary government. I go along with all this but I'd like to add that trial by jury is also a last resort. For one thing, it is very expensive. Not every client can afford it. For another, a jury is unpredictable; you gamble on it only when you have to.

A trial by jury was necessary in the case of Richie Alston.

Twenty-five-year-old Richard Alston stood accused of the murder of two men. He was accused of participating with others in a kind of "gangland execution." And, frankly, the DA had a strong case against him. The DA wasn't interested in any plea bargaining, in any compromise "deals." He was sure he was going to nail Alston on two charges of first degree and put him away for life.

When a DA feels like that, a defendant's only hope is a jury of his peers. Oh, we could have waived a jury and asked a judge to make the decision. But in a tough case, a judge will rarely ignore the DA's evidence. In fact, in a really tough case, a judge may order a jury trial even if the defendant is willing to waive one.

Richie Alston's story begins in 1970 with the formation in Philadelphia of a group called the People's Liberation Army. The PLA is a black revolutionary organization, linked philosophically, if not in any other way, to the Symbionese Liberation Army (SLA) of California and the Black Liberation Army of New York.

As best the police have been able to determine, the PLA was organized by a mysterious Oriental named Sulieman Abdur Rahim. There is some doubt as to where this Sulieman came from, and at this writing, even greater doubt as to where he has gone. But in the summer of 1970 he came to live in West Oak Lane, an integrated, middle-class Philadelphia neighborhood, and opened a karate school there. Sulieman was then thirty-four years old, a tall, muscular man with a constantly changing appearance. Sometimes he appeared with shaved head, sometimes with a wig. Sometimes he had a moustache, other times not. He told those who were attracted to him that he was an agent from Red China, that he'd been a bodyguard of Malcolm X, that he'd fought with Ché Guevara, that he'd killed two CIA agents. Most importantly, he said he had come to Philadelphia with a mission—a mission to "build the revolution," to "liberate oppressed peoples."

Philadelphia must have seemed a good territory for revolution-building—particularly that year.

The early sixties were the years of civil-rights marches,

sit-ins, and voter-registration drives. The mid-sixties were the years of ghetto riots and growing impatience, particularly on the part of young black people, with white society's fear of change. By the late sixties, black protest had grown increasing militant. And the Black Panthers could make White America uptight just by saying, "Death to the pigs" or "Power to the people" . . . they didn't even have to *do* anything.

The summer of 1970 was a particularly uneasy one in Philadelphia. Three policemen had been shot and if the accused murderers were not Black Panthers, the police obviously felt that Panther rhetoric was partly responsible for the tragedy. So there was a shoot-'em-up raid on a Black Panther headquarters—a row house in a ghetto. The inhabitants of the house were forced onto the sidewalk to be searched. The next day, the tabloid *Daily News* carried a picture of six Panthers—their hands against the wall—*stark naked*. In addition, the police commissioner had referred to Panthers as "yellow dogs."

Feelings ran high, to put it mildly. And it was into this tense, angry, polarized community that Sulieman Abdur Rahim brought his message of revolt.

He gathered a clique of followers around him. From a briefcase dramatically locked with a padlock, Sulieman would produce documents which, he claimed, outlined a government plot called the "King Alfred Plan" to stir up ghetto riots and then lock all blacks in concentration camps and exterminate them.

Sulieman did not bother to mention that the "King Alfred Plan" was fictional—that it had been lifted whole from page 306 of a novel, *The Man Who Cried I Am*, by John A. Williams. But he did show them a book called *Concentration Camps, U.S.A.*, which discussed the six

camps that were established in the United States under
the McCarran Act during the Communist scare of the
1950s and never used. He passed out handbooks on police
tactics, guerrilla warfare, and revolutionary doctrine.

And each listener, not unfamiliar with examples of
racism, sensitive to the hostile mood of the white community, and nursing his or her own personal hurts and
disappointments, found something in what Sulieman was
saying.

The PLA was not a poverty-stricken or stupid group.
They were, in fact, middle class and intelligent. Richard
Stewart, thirty-eight, a plumber, was well read in authors
from novelist Ernest Hemingway to anarchist Emma Gold-
berg. Stewart was a moving force in the organization.

There was Lee Jenkins, a laboratory technician, nick-
named "the professor" because he had been to college.
Ken Tervalon, twenty-four, was an insurance under-
writer. Ray Crawford, twenty-two, had just returned from
a tour of duty as a helicopter pilot in Vietnam. Leonidas
Brown, nineteen, managed a small dry-cleaning shop.
Ronald Murray, twenty-five, was an electrician.

Willie Williams, eighteen, was a hospital employee
and the son of a disabled policeman. Roger Conway,
twenty, was in the Navy and stationed at the Philadelphia
Naval Hospital. Donald Dowd, twenty-two, operated a
fork lift. Richie Alston, twenty-one, was a credit clerk
and part-time college student. Kevin Hall and Mervin
Childs, both eighteen, had just graduated from high
school. Philip Wormley, twenty-six, was unemployed and
lived with his girlfriend. I never found out what Billy
Lott, twenty-one, did.

There were probably others whose names, as well as
occupations, I don't know.

Leonidas Brown's father was a member of a shooting lodge—a legitimate sporting club—in the Pocono Mountains north of Allentown, Pennsylvania. Soon Sulieman and his followers arranged to practice marksmanship at the lodge. The shooting that Sulieman had in mind, of course, had nothing to do with sport. He thought the PLA should buy more weapons and make bombs. But to do this, they needed money.

And so, on November 7, 1970, they robbed a Gino's Restaurant—one of a chain of fast hamburger places. Kevin Hall had gotten a job there to case the place.

From the PLA point of view, they were "liberating" capital from the capitalists. While nine men stood outside and two waited in cars, Philip Wormley and William Lott entered the restaurant. "No one is going to get hurt," Wormley said. "We are taking money for the People's Liberation Army." The heist went off smoothly and they got away with three thousand dollars.

Two weeks later, on the night of November 20, Sulieman convened a "People's Revolutionary Court"—to charge that Wormley and his friend, Ronald Murray, had not turned over all the proceeds of the Gino's holdup to the PLA. He said he'd found out that the two had kept some of the money, invested it in drugs, and had given drugs to some of the young members. He accused the two of subverting the aims of the organization. Wormley and Murray were not present to defend themselves.

A vote was taken. Around the table, each man put out his hand—thumbs down—except Richard Stewart, who made his vote just as plain another way. Stewart had been cleaning a gun—he picked it up, pointed it, and said, "This is how I vote."

The matter was turned over to a "security squad" for

disposition. Richard Stewart says he was a member of that security squad, but just who were the other members—and who were the men around the table "conducting court"—have been matters of dispute in various trials.

Wormley and Murray were shot the next night. Murray was shot as he lay in bed in his apartment. Wormley was taken outside his apartment and shot in an alley. Autopsies showed Wormley had been hit seven times, Murray twelve.

The "security squad" thought they'd left both men dead. Stewart told of taking their pulses, tears in his eyes, and finding none.

But Murray was not dead . . . yet. He staggered out of his house and was spotted by a policeman. "I'm bleeding . . . I've been shot," he said. A police wagon arrived in lieu of an ambulance. Murray was put inside by himself. At the hospital, he was able to climb out and onto a stretcher.

He died three days later.

Before he died, he gave six statements to the police. The police said that first Murray would say only, "There were four of them." Murray said he could not give the names but that Philip would give them the story. Philip who? Philip Wormley.

The police said Murray opened up after he was told, "You are going to die; give us the names of those who got you."

The police claimed that Murray named Richard Alston five times. He also mentioned Roger Conway; a "Duall," whom they later decided was Donald Dowd; "Crow," which was said to be a nickname for Ray Crawford; and "Dickie," a nickname for Richard Stewart.

Wormley's girlfriend said she recognized Ken Tervalon as the man who came to the door and demanded that "Chopper" come outside. She led police to Tervalon's house.

Roger Conway, arrested at the Navy hospital, gave police a statement, denying involvement in the murders. He wasn't on the security squad; he said he was the "propaganda chief." If the organization ever got a printing press, he was supposed to operate it. But it didn't have a printing press, so he didn't do anything.

He said that he was at Sulieman's having dinner when "Leon [meaning Leonidas Brown], Dickie, Richard, and Dowd" had come by to report they had "dealt with 'Snooky,'" which was Murray's nickname, and were on the way to get "Chopper," which was Wormley's nickname.

Naturally, the police set out to arrest everybody who was named by anybody—either as prosecutor at the "trial" (Sulieman Abdur Rahim), as carry-outer of the sentence (Alston, Dowd, Brown, Crawford, Stewart, Conway, Tervalon), or as a participant in the Gino's caper (Hall, Lott, Williams, Jenkins, and Childs).

Some were picked up quite easily. Jenkins, "the professor," came to the police. He just happened to be reading a book he'd picked up—*The Man Who Cried I Am*— and lo, discovered the "King Alfred Plan" had been a hoax. Furious at having been tricked, Jenkins walked in talking.

Donald Dowd and Sulieman Rahim went to Georgia. Dowd was arrested in a hotel lobby there when an employee spotted him carrying a gun. By the time the police learned that Dowd's companion was wanted by police too, Sulieman had taken off.

Billy Lott disappeared. Alston and Stewart were arrested more than a year and a half later—Alston in his girlfriend's apartment in Philadelphia, Stewart in Canada.

The shootings had occurred on a Sunday night. Richard Alston went to his job at the Atlantic-Richfield Company on Monday morning as usual. However, when the company's security chief told him that the police were on their way there to see him, Alston took off—running down thirteen flights of stairs.

Alston went only as far as his apartment. But there, Stewart found him. Stewart went to get Alston when he heard Murray was still alive and advised Alston to come with him. Stewart and Alston remained in the city—undiscovered—for ten days and then left on a cross-country tour. Stewart had contacts with Liberation Army people everywhere. Money was no problem because Stewart's contacts provided housing and food and whatever else the fugitives wanted.

They returned to Philadelphia in January and remained—once again undiscovered—until March. Then Stewart, Alston, and Alston's white girlfriend, whom we shall call Stephanie Court, decided to go to Canada. After ten months Stephanie returned to Philadelphia. Alston followed a few months later. It was in Stephanie's apartment that Alston was found and arrested by the FBI.

The fact that Alston was out of the country for a considerable period of time had an important bearing on his case and on the kind of defense strategy I developed for it. Most importantly, it affected the order in which the various trials took place.

If Alston had not fled the country, he probably would have been tried first. Usually, if there is to be a series of trials involving the same crime, the prosecutor will attempt to proceed with his strongest case first. Once you get a conviction, it can have a domino effect on those still awaiting trial. They, as well as the convicted defendant, may decide to turn state's evidence or they may decide to go for a plea.

I know that the assistant DA who handled all these cases, Tony Bateman, felt he had the strongest case with Alston. There were those deathbed statements in which —according to the police—Alston was named five times. The fact that Alston ran the minute he heard the police were coming to see him might convince a jury he had a "guilty conscience." Alston drove a dark-maroon fastback and such an automobile had been seen screeching away from the Wormley murder scene. Furthermore, when the police got a warrant to search Alston's house, they recovered rifles, ammunition, scopes, and rifle slings.

But Bateman went with Conway first because, I suppose, he felt he also had a good case against him . . . and because Conway was available. There are, of course, certain logistic problems that affect the order of trial: which defendant has had his preliminary hearing, which detectives are available for trial versus which ones are on vacation, which lawyer has gotten his fee and is willing to proceed versus which one is stalling until the client's family comes up with the money.

Conway was charged with murder and conspiracy. His lawyer played around with the six alleged deathbed statements. Conway had been named in two of the six, but he wasn't named at first. When he was named, another name—Alston's—was left off. The lawyer managed to create a reasonable doubt with this.

"There is no doubt about Alston," he intoned to the jury, "but Conway is a different story."

Probably what the jury decided to do was compromise. They weren't convinced Conway had been the murderer, but they did think he was mixed up in it all somehow. So they convicted him of conspiracy while acquitting him of murder. The judge then sentenced him to the time already served, and since Conway had already spent eighteen months in jail awaiting trial, he just went home.

Another eighteen months and four more trials passed before my client's—Alston's—trial came up. Alston was taken into custody shortly before the Conway trial was in progress and the DA wanted to try his case next. But I was able to obtain a delay by arguing that the four others, who had been in custody almost two years at that point, should be tried first. I said I felt it was only fair to give them a chance to win their freedom in advance of Alston, who had been free all that time as a fugitive. The court agreed.

Obviously, I wanted to postpone Alston's trial as long as possible even though my client would have to wait out that delay in jail.

The oath every attorney takes when admitted to the bar includes a line that he or she "shall delay no man's cause for lucre or malice." But the delay in Alston's case was not for my benefit, but for his. Every trial that took place before his give me a chance to gain new information about the case, information I would try to use on Richie Alston's behalf.

Leonidas Brown was tried next and acquitted. His own testimony, I think, was his best defense, plus the fact that he had not been named by Murray at any time. It was true that police found arms at his home, but Brown could show that guns were his hobby. His father had belonged to that gun club in the mountains and first took Leonidas there when he was only six.

Tervalon, Dowd, and Crawford were convicted of first-degree murder. Wormley's girlfriend testified against Tervalon. The other two had been named by Murray. And it probably did not help any of the three with the juries that none of them took the stand in their own defense. Unfortunately for them, all three had previously either made an incriminating statement or appeared in an incriminating situation which their attorneys felt was best left uncross-examined. They were, in a sense, damned if they took the stand and damned if they didn't.

The major witness for the state in each trial was Willie Williams, the hospital worker and policeman's son, who since that fateful summer had joined the Army. Obviously, Willie had made a deal to testify for the commonwealth if no charges were placed against him. And obviously, too, Willie Williams was more afraid of what the commonwealth *could* do to him than of what his erstwhile colleagues might *want* to do to him.

During the Brown trial, Williams testified that he had received a threatening letter. He said it looked like Sulieman's handwriting:

> Dear Brother . . . I am safe at this time, but I will be back. I hear people are looking for you. They have something you don't. They have time. Lots of time. So, stay paranoid. Keep looking over your shoulder. . . . You have betrayed innocent brothers. You have lied to save yourself. But there are many of us. . . . You only betrayed a few cells. Thank God you didn't know more. You would have betrayed the whole revolution. Entimio [a man said to have betrayed Castro in the Cuban Revolution] is remembered. Count the days before we meet again.
> Captain 35

I was busy on Alston's behalf all through the other trials. I was busy collecting testimony and I went to every other attorney to ask them to give me what they had . . . and in return I'd pass on what I had.

"I don't think you have the notes of testimony on Brown's preliminary hearing. Do you have Conway's statement?" Etc., etc. I'd pop in to each trial . . . just in and out in ten minutes . . . giving away documents and collecting them.

The more trials that preceded Alston's, the more testimony I collected, the happier I was. I prepared a master index showing the names of all witnesses who had testified at all other proceedings, at preliminary hearings, at pretrial hearings on the admissibility of evidence, at bail hearings, and, of course, at the key trials. The most difficult one to index was Willie Williams, because he consumed hundreds of pages at each trial.

My first major digest of his testimony alone was twenty-seven pages, listing the specific proceeding and the page number. But twenty-seven pages is still too long. When you cross-examine somebody, you can't flip through twenty-seven pages to find the right quote unless you're willing to put the jury to sleep. So I made a digest of my digest. I listed the Williams testimony by topics: robbery of Gino's, Wednesday meeting after the robbery, shooting of Wormley, etc. Then I made a digest of the digest of the digest with the most pertinent and crucial parts marked in different colors.

This was done for every witness who had ever testified—for every police officer—so that when they took the stand at Alston's trial and made a statement, I would be able to know right away if they had contradicted something they had said before—if they had made a mistake.

I had gotten copies of police reports from the other lawyers after they had been introduced as evidence in the other trials, and so if an officer took the stand and said he didn't have a particular report with him, I produced it for him. That makes points for the defense every time.

Most of the work at any trial is not done at the trial. That's only the tip of the iceberg. In some ways, the trial is anticlimactic.

Besides worrying about the trials of others that preceded Alston's trial, I worried about the various hearings for Alston that preceded Alston's trial.

I waived a preliminary hearing for him. The preliminary hearing merely gives the DA the opportunity to establish a *prima facie* (Latin for "at first appearance") case—that it's "probable" the accused did it. And the defense is usually anxious to have the prelim because it is its first discovery shot. The defense doesn't have to show its hand, but it can try to get in as much cross-examination as possible to find out what the DA has in his hand. You want to know the key witnesses; you want to sniff out any possibilities for suppression of arrest or evidence or statement.

In Alston's case, however, I already had that information. In this case, therefore, the preliminary hearing was a potential liability. If once a witness goes on record under oath—and is cross-examined—that testimony can be used at a trial even if the witness drops dead walking from the hearing room. On the other hand, if a witness for the commonwealth should have a change of heart, have a heart attack, or somehow die before the trial—and that witness is *never* on record testifying against the accused—well, the accused is a lot better off.

Besides, I didn't want to remind Bateman, the assistant DA, too forcibly of my client's existence. I didn't want to bother him with additional hearings—let him concentrate on nailing everybody else.

Like every other client I have ever had, Alston's first words to me were: "Can you get me out on bail?" The answer to that was no. The law says that bail is permissible in every case unless the court determines the accused might become a fugitive. And Alston had been a fugitive.

I tried anyway.

At the bail hearing, the DA went to work to convict Alston of an entirely new crime. He claimed that while Stewart and Alston were in Canada they'd joined a revolutionary movement there, robbed a bank, and shot a Mountie.

I protested that. Stewart may have been arrested in Canada, but Alston had been in jail in Philadelphia for months at that point and no charge had been placed against him by Canadian authorities for anything.

The judge set bail at $100,000, which meant Alston had to come up with $10,000—10 percent—to get bail bond; he couldn't, so he stayed in jail until he was tried—a year and a half.

The next pretrial step is the suppression hearing. I sought to suppress everything. It doesn't hurt to try.

I moved to quash one indictment on the grounds that I'd never waived a preliminary hearing on it. I had noticed when I signed the waivers that both papers I signed had only Murray's name on them. I didn't call it to anybody's attention at the time. But I thought the suppression hearing was a good time to mention it. Bateman called my action "trickiness." And then he met "trickiness" with more trickiness because somehow or other he produced a waiver with Wormley's name on it. Hmmm.

I also sought to suppress the weapons that had been taken from Alston's home and his car. The police found hunting rifles, shotguns, and telescope attachments in the Alston basement and a pistol in his car.

I asked the court to rule that all these weapons had been found as a result of an improper police search and therefore they could not be mentioned at Alston's trial (the less mention of firearms, the better, I thought). But I lost.

Actually, I expected to lose. I felt there was probable cause for arrest. I felt the search of Alston's car and home and the removal of weapons from them had been done quite properly. But the suppression hearing gave me an opportunity to probe the evidence against him.

I had bypassed the preliminary hearing because I hadn't felt I would learn much there, but I definitely wasn't going to bypass any other opportunities. In a civil case, each side knows what the other side has got before the trial—there have been discovery interviews, depositions, pleadings, and interrogatories. But in a criminal case, the only thing the DA is required to reveal before trial is a confession by the defendant. Whatever a defense attorney can learn through pretrial hearings is a plus.

I was a court-appointed attorney for Alston. (I'd been hired privately at first, but the family ran out of money.) The court didn't have to appoint me, but I guess the judge felt it would save money in the long run not to force a new attorney to redo the work I'd already done. Being court-appointed gave me the opportunity to learn a little more about the DA's case.

I'd have to go into court every time I wanted money for something. I assumed that the DA would have an expert to prove that certain bullets in a body came from a gun taken from Stewart in Canada or from a gun taken from

Dowd in Georgia. So I applied for a ballistician who might make separate comparisons for the defense. And naturally I asked in court for the DA's ballistics reports to show that I would need an expert to testify about them.

Well, it developed I didn't hire a ballistician. I'm not going to use public money to fight futile battles. But the way I learned that the fight would be futile was by getting a look at the DA's reports.

I learned something very helpful at the suppression hearing—that I'd better not try to call Alston's mother as a defense witness. She testified at the suppression hearing that she knew her son was in "bad trouble." If she took the witness stand at the trial, the DA would be sure to remind her of that statement.

So instead of bringing Alston's parents in to testify, I asked them to come to court, sit in the front row, and "root." I explained to the jury that Richie Alston was giving up his right to call his parents as witnesses so that they might sit through the entire trial. A witness is generally barred from the courtroom until called to testify so that his or her testimony will not be influenced by what other witnesses have said. (Happily, Bateman did not mess me up by graciously permitting the parents to both watch the trial and testify.)

Pretrial maneuvers do not end with pretrial hearings.

I wanted, if I could, to determine who the judge would be and when the trial would be held; I also wanted to be sure that the jury would not be locked up. Sometimes these matters are entirely beyond the defense attorney's power to do more than hope for, but they aren't matters to be overlooked either.

I particularly wanted Judge Jim McDermott to sit on this case.

Judge McDermott is not usually a defense attorney's

favorite judge. He is beloved, rather, by the district attorney's office because he is a "tough" judge. And I didn't think I'd get much of a fight from the DA's office if I tried to get the Alston trial on his calendar.

There were several reasons I wanted McDermott. One was that he was familiar with the case. He'd presided at both the Conway and Tervalon trials. The other reason was that I thought this judge might see a dimension in the killings of Wormley and Murray that another judge might not. McDermott has no love for murderers of any stripe, but, at the same time, he has no love for drug-pushers either. He really hates drug-pushers. A couple of weeks before the Alston trial, Judge McDermott sentenced a sixty-year-old man to a sixteen-year prison sentence, and when the defense attorney objected that the judge was condemning this man to die in prison, McDermott said only: "so be it." Because the man had sold drugs.

The defense was contending that Murray and Wormley had been killed—not by Alston—but killed because they had bought and sold drugs. The DA would say it was just because they had taken some of the Gino's money for themselves, but we would have testimony that they were killed not for taking the money but for the manner in which they used it. Judge McDermott would be able to see things in the light which we planned to shine.

So I asked the calendar judge if the case could be assigned to McDermott. I personally promised McDermott an interesting trial if he'd take the case, and we got McDermott.

Next, by dint of being busy on other cases a little earlier, I was not available for trial until just before Christmas. I would prefer a jury in a good-will-toward-men frame of mind. It was also for this reason that I didn't want them locked up. Every one of the other five trials had sequestered the jury, and that's tough on people. Night and day, the jurors are in the custody of court officers. Every time they go to a restaurant or a movie, they are with each other—and the court officers. They are not allowed to read newspapers or murder mysteries, or watch news or crime shows on TV. They worry about their families (they may not even phone them), their jobs, their businesses. They send hysterical letters to the judge; I saw some when I was in the DA's office.

A locked-up jury can get annoyed and upset at whichever side seems to be prolonging the trial. But, all things being equal, I think a locked-up jury leans toward the prosecution. They feel they are "drafted into service"— and it isn't necessarily the defense they are serving.

Anyway, I wanted a relaxed, attentive jury, and I thought they'd be more interested if they weren't worrying about when they would get their Christmas shopping done. Apparently the judge agreed.

(Locked-up juries used to be automatic on murder cases, but they are so expensive—housing, feeding, guarding, and entertaining fourteen people for weeks—that locking them up has become discretionary with the judge.)

Only one thing more was necessary to make the setting of the Alston trial perfect: an exhausted DA—and we had that too. Tony Bateman was the logical person to prosecute, since he had handled all the other trials. And poor Tony had just concluded a six-week trial with hard-hitting defense attorney Cecil Moore (about whom more later). What Tony needed after six weeks of being harassed and insulted by Moore was a couple of weeks on a beach in Miami; what he got was Alston and me.

Did I gallantly agree to put off the trial a few days to give Tony a well-deserved rest? Of course not—I'm not crazy.

And so, three years after the shootings, one and a half years after Alston's arrest, after months of hearings, hasslings, and frantic footwork, in the second week of December 1973, the case of *Commonwealth vs. Richard Alston* was on.

Judge McDermott was on the bench. Some seventy citizens who were potential jurors were seated in the courtroom waiting for jury selection to begin.

Bateman moved to go to trial on the indictment of murder alone. He did not want to give this jury the opportunity the Conway jury had had of compromising on the lesser indictment of conspiracy rather than knocking heads on the question of murder. I jumped up and moved that the trial proceed on both indictments.

The judge, very properly, rebuked me.

"Mr. Moldovsky, it is up to the district attorney to decide what he is moving for trial on."

It is . . . but it won't hurt the defense if all those potential jurors sitting there hear that the prosecution doesn't want to let them decide everything, that he is holding something back. The defense is willing to place everything in their hands, but the DA is not.

We proceeded to jury selection—twelve jurors and two alternates.

Now, I know a lot of attorneys make a real mystique out of jury selection, and I don't knock it. If the defense has a psychologist on its side who can pick out those people most likely to be biased in its favor, that's just one more weapon in the old arsenal. Some attorneys feel they can psyche out people on their own. One man will never select a woman who wears a hat, another will never take a man who chews gum—that kind of thing.

I'm inclined to accept the luck of the draw most of the time. Oh, if the prospective juror doesn't look me in the eye when I ask a few questions, but then smiles at the DA, I'll certainly strike him from the list. But if somebody gives me a straight, open answer, I'm inclined to go along and hope for the best. Because you just never know what's going on in a juror's mind.

You may think somebody is a real law-and-order type, a real police booster, and then one day on the way to the courtroom, a cop gives him a ticket for speeding—and presto, he's now antagonistic to all police witnesses.

In my opening speech to the jurors, I pleaded with them: "Do not unjustly condemn Richard Alston to life in a cage."

A lot of defense attorneys postpone their opening speech until after the prosecution has presented its case. That way they aren't sandbagged by any prosecution surprises. They then address the jury just before putting on the defense case. But I like to do what I can at the outset, to condition the jury to listen to the prosecution case with some of the defense point of view in mind.

I stressed the idea in my opening that Alston was falsely accused, unjustly on trial. "Ladies and gentlemen of the jury, you will learn that Richard Alston was not a member of the People's Liberation Army. Oh, he was being recruited. They liked him. But he was not a participant in any PLA activity. . . ."

And just as I had promised Judge McDermott an interesting trial, I promised the same to the jury. I told them that in this trial they would hear Richard Stewart take the stand to confess the murders—to condemn himself—in an effort to see that a man falsely accused does not spend the rest of his life in jail.

That's a risky promise to make. If Stewart, who had promised me he would testify, changed his mind, the jury might well react in disappointment against the entire defense case. But I was sure about Stewart.

Stewart wrote me a letter from jail asking me to come see him. Stewart, a tall, good-looking bearded man, is a real honest-to-God revolutionary. He defines himself as an officer in charge of a guerrilla army at war with a society that is oppressive to the black and the poor. In shooting Wormley and Murray, he was only "maintaining discipline in the ranks"—dealing with deserters and traitors—as an officer at war must, distasteful though the task may be.

"The execution of my two comrades is a burden I carry with me," he said.

Stewart considers himself a prisoner of war; he even lettered "P.O.W." on his prison uniform.

When I met Stewart I was convinced I was not in the presence of any put-on. Stewart believed in what he was doing, and if Stewart said he wanted to talk about the People's Liberation Army and he wanted to help Alston, I could believe he'd do it.

The police and the DA, though, couldn't believe Stewart was really going to tell all and they tried to build up pressure by accelerating the date of his suppression hearing. They expected him to demand his rights to suppress his statements. But much to their shock and surprise, Stewart said he didn't want anything suppressed.

Stewart was truly taking his life in his hands. At the

time of the murders capital punishment was legal. By the time of the Alston trial, the Supreme Court had ruled that it was illegal the way it was then handled. Pennsylvania and many other states later passed new capital-punishment laws to meet Supreme Court guidelines. Thus Stewart, who was warned that by the time he came to trial capital punishment would probably be enforced again, was indeed doing something incredible.

After that suppression hearing, the DA didn't want me talking to Stewart any more. Four highway patrolmen were assigned to keep him in continuous custody. I went up to the cellroom (where prisoners who are scheduled for a court appearance are kept during the day) to see him (with his attorney's permission), and these patrolmen locked hands so that the sheriff's men couldn't bring him out to see me.

The sheriffs apologized and said it wasn't their fault. I then got a court order from McDermott ordering them to let me see Stewart, but I neglected to get him to say for how long. So I got to see him for exactly thirty seconds and he was whisked away. "We complied with the court order," said one of the patrolmen.

They were putting pressure on Alston in jail, too. Alston had a sinus condition that required medication; without it he kept blowing his nose. And his medication was cut off. I could have explained to the jury that my man was blowing his nose all the time because he couldn't get his medicine, but the jury might think I was just making up an explanation to cover my client's nervous behavior. Once again, Judge McDermott signed an order, this time restoring Alston's medicine, and Alston was okay by the time he testified.

I didn't waste any time getting Stewart onto the stand. As soon as Bateman rested his case, I called Stewart as my first witness.

Stewart had a pretty good audience in the courtroom besides the jury. Word spread around City Hall that a witness in Room 653 was going to pull a Perry Mason and confess on the stand. And City Hall employees, lawyers between hearings, reporters, and whoever else was around dropped in to listen.

Stewart delivered as promised.

"I did the killings," he said.

"I walked in [to Murray's bedroom]. There was a psychedelic light in the room. He was lying on the bed. I had a flashlight. I shined it in his face. He flipped his eyes and I saw he was probably taking acid. He shouted, 'What are you guys doing?' I turned the radio all the way up. Snooky [Murray] lay down and put his arm across his eyes. He knew what was happening. Then the shooting began."

A scream rent the courtroom. Murray's mother had been sitting there. She began to sob and ran out of the room. You could hear the screams going down the hallway.

"I'm sorry about that lady," Stewart continued placidly. "I feel as bad as she does . . . but that's life. When the shooting was over, as captain of the squad, it was my duty to fire a shot into his brain.

"I said goodbye to Snooky, but the gun clicked [and didn't fire]. I found I was emotional. I really liked Snooky. I didn't realize I was crying and I was glad I didn't wind up putting a bullet in his brain."

After the shooting of Murray, Stewart testified, the squad had proceeded to Wormley's. Stewart remained in the car while the others went into the house and brought Wormley to the alley.

"'Finish Wormley,' I said," Stewart related. "Wormley was executed. I fired a final bullet into his brain."

Unlike the Perry Mason plots, the fact that Stewart said he did do it didn't automatically prove my client did not. Because, after all, there were supposed to be at least four members of the squad. Stewart, naturally, was asked to name the other three.

He would not. He contended they were from New York and he knew them only by first names or nicknames, and all he could say was that Alston was not among them —nor, he added, were Dowd, Tervalon, Conway, or Crawford.

Stewart was perfectly willing to confess to murder but not to answer just any old question put to him.

Stewart had said he became a revolutionary after attending "underground lectures" three nights a week for six months. Bateman then asked Stewart for the names and addresses of those who had attended the lectures with him. Stewart did not reply.

"I'm prepared to wait for your answer," said Bateman.

"I'm prepared to die," said Stewart.

Bateman's question had no bearing on the murders but on Stewart's credibility. Bateman wanted to show the jury that Stewart chose to hide some things.

Judge McDermott had a time with Stewart. "Do you understand," the judge asked Stewart, "you have been asked to name the people who were with you in New York?"

"Oh, yes, I understand," said Stewart.

"Do you understand, Mr. Stewart, that I have ruled you must answer?"

"Oh, yes, I understand, sir."

"Are you telling me that you refuse to answer what I have ordered you to answer?"

"Oh, yes, sir, I am, sir."

McDermott could have sentenced Stewart to five hundred years for contempt the way Stewart was refusing to answer. Or McDermott could have ordered Stewart's entire testimony struck from the record. A rule of law says that if a witness won't answer questions on cross-examination, his direct testimony can be disregarded. Bateman realized that striking Stewart's words from the record would not strike them from the jurors' minds, but it might influence the jury, certainly, to hear the judge order them struck.

Judge McDermott, however, decided to allow the testimony to stand. The jury had heard Stewart answer and also his refusal to answer. The jury could decide how to take him.

In the Alston trial, as in the previous trials, the DA's major witness was Willie Williams. In my pretrial preparations, reading and digesting the testimony in each trial, I began to get a psychological feel for each witness. I noticed that when Willie Williams was cornered on his relationship with Sulieman—Sulieman whispering in his ear, Sulieman asking him to stick around—then his testimony about the PLA was wild.

"They said they were going to kill the pigs, blow up the roundhouse [police headquarters] . . . it was violence all over the place."

But if asked about the purposes of the organization with no personalities involved, there was a different response: "Oh, I'm not sure. Some people talked about kidnapping the police chief, but that wasn't serious."

In my preparation, I got to know in what sequence to

ask which question, what topics to cover to get specific results. I could not have known that if the Alston trial had gone on first, or if it had been the only trial.

I knew Willie Williams well enough after reading all those transcripts to take risks the defense attorneys in the early trials would not have dared take.

For instance, when I was cross-examining Williams, I asked him to step from the stand and write the names of all the people who had participated in the Gino's robbery.

I like to use demonstrative evidence where I can. In a criminal case, it's usually the commonwealth that has guns and pictures of bloody bodies to wave around. If you can produce a little movement you might even wake up those jurors who have fallen asleep.

Bateman had questioned Williams for an hour and a half. I got him late in the afternoon. I asked him questions that I knew wouldn't upset him, and I then took my risk.

I produced a blackboard for Williams to write upon. He wrote down thirteen names. He did not include the names of Richie Alston or Leonidas Brown. Obviously, I knew from reading prior testimony that he had never named Alston in the Gino's heist. The DA would claim that anybody who even helped plan the robbery was involved in it, even if he wasn't actually on the scene, but that wouldn't be how Willie Williams would see it.

Williams went back to the witness stand.

"Take a good look. Have you forgotten anyone?"

"No."

"Where are the names of Richard Alston and Leonidas Brown, if they participated?"

Williams jumped down from the stand and wrote in their names.

"Why did you put those names down?"

"Because they planned it."

"Do you have a distinct recollection of Alston and Brown at the meeting at which the robbery was planned?" (I knew from back testimony that Williams thought "distinct recollection" meant something more specific than "do you remember?")

"No, I don't have a distinct recollection."

"Then, in all fairness, we should remove their names." I erased them.

Bateman, on redirect, had Williams say again that Alston and Brown had helped plan the robbery, and put the names back on the blackboard. And I, on recross, got him to admit again he had no "distinct recollection" and took them off again.

I think that this erasing of the names had an effect on the jury.

Obviously, if Williams had written Alston's name on the list from the first, my strategy would have backfired. I was counting on all my preparation to come through for me—and it did.

I can't stress enough the importance of knowing what had been said before. I could predict, then, what would be said later.

A policeman who had sat next to Murray's bed in the hospital testified that Murray had mentioned Alston's name. The policeman said he had written the name on the bedsheet in order to get the correct spelling. At an earlier trial, the officer had been asked to produce the bedsheet; he said he didn't have it because a nurse had chased him from the room.

When that same officer faced our jury and repeated the story, I immediately asked him for the sheet.

"I don't have it."

I was stunned, shocked, surprised, and amazed.

"You don't *have* it?"

When Bateman didn't call Detective William Morris to the stand for the prosecution, I knew that I should call him for the defense. Morris had spent sixteen hours with Murray before Murray had died. Eight hours one day, eight hours the next. He had taken two statements from him, and neither statement contained the name of Richard Alston.

Bateman presented those policemen who had taken statements from Murray that did mention Alston. I attacked them by making a fuss over the medical reports, which showed Murray had a bullet wound in the mouth, teeth had been shot away, his upper palate fractured, and his tongue was partially severed. How could they be sure what Murray was saying? Certainly Murray was in no shape to enunciate clearly. Maybe when they thought he was saying Richard Alston, he was really saying Richard Stewart.

Bateman countered by presenting evidence to show that in a matter of hours and particularly within a day or two of his admission to the hospital, Murray's condition had begun to stabilize and his speech had become more understandable.

That was exactly what I wanted Bateman to do. And then I presented the detective who had been with Murray the longest period of time, and the *last* period of time. When, if you could believe the DA, Murray's speech must have been at its clearest, Alston's name was not mentioned.

When I called Detective Morris as my witness, Bateman was on his feet immediately. "Objection. Objection!"

I was delighted. The jury could not help but notice that

the DA wanted them to hear six policemen testify about deathbed statements but not the seventh policeman, who had been with Murray the longest time.

You just know how a jury is going to feel about that. Poor Tony. I had mentioned that he was tired.

Police testimony, of course, was important to this case, so I kept all my digests of police testimony at the ready. And I was able to point out to the jury even the smallest changes in police testimony. At one trial Murray is quoted as saying "three or four colored guys"; at the next trial it became "four black guys"; at the next, "black males"; at the next, "three or four in a white Chevy."

I elicited from the policemen who took Murray to the hospital that no one had ridden in the back of the wagon with him. That had no bearing on the case except perhaps to give the jury the image of the police as people who would let a gravely wounded man roll around on a hard bench by himself on the way to the hospital.

I tried a lot of things in the Alston trial that the defense attorneys in the other trials had not attempted. But then I felt justified in trying new things because I could see from the records that other things hadn't helped.

For the most part, the other counsel relied on trying to impeach the testimony of Willie Williams. And I didn't overlook that either.

Under cross-examination, I got Willie to admit that he'd taken a lot of LSD in the summer of 1970. I hoped to get across the idea that if Willie was an acid freak, his memory of what had occurred wouldn't be too reliable.

Stewart told some terrible tales about Willie. He said Willie had asked him to help murder his (Willie's) father. ("We don't get involved in domestic quarrels," said Stewart.) He said Willie had volunteered to sneak into Murray's room with his hospital uniform and pull all the tubes from Murray's arms. Willie, of course, hotly denied these stories, but it was up to the jury to decide who to believe.

A complication in the Alston case not present in any of the others was Alston's girlfriend, because she was white. There are those who would be willing to convict a black man just for having a white girlfriend and nothing else.

Stephanie had fled with Richie to Canada, taking two years' savings with her. Richie had been arrested in her apartment. In fact, she was charged as an accessory. I had hoped, and so had her attorney, that she would be able to take the Fifth Amendment at the Alston trial. But the DA outflanked that maneuver by getting a judge to give Stephanie immunity from prosecution. She couldn't incriminate herself if she had immunity.

So she had to testify—and that made me very nervous. But, in the end, I don't think she helped Bateman's case at all. She told the jury that she loved Richie Alston, that he was a wonderful person. She said she had convinced him to take her to Canada and that her savings had only been used for her own expenses, not his. He had taken odd jobs to support himself.

And finally, she testified that Richie had told her he had only attended meetings. "If he had been involved with anything else, he would have told me."

Alston took the stand to explain to the jury why he had fled from his job when he heard the police were coming there and why he later left the city with Stewart. Needless to say, the prosecution made the most of his fugitive status. If he wasn't guilty of a crime, why did he feel the need to run?

Alston said he thought the police were going to accuse him of a crime, all right, but the crime involved was a minor one—parking violation. Alston maintained he thought the police were going to arrest him on a scofflaw traffic warrant. Alston had failed to pay a half-dozen traffic tickets and, in addition, had left his car in a no-parking area again that morning. He told the jury he ran from the building to move his car and also to go to the bank and get cash in order to post bond for the traffic warrant.

When Stewart came to his apartment, he related, he learned for the first time of the shootings. Stewart did not then tell him that he'd been involved. But he did say that the police were bound to suspect all of them and that for their own protection, they'd best keep out of sight. Alston said he relied completely on Stewart's judgment. If he had any doubts at first, he added, they were laid to rest as the newspapers recounted the arrests of the others.

Both versions were plausible ones: that Alston had fled because he knew he was guilty and also that Alston had fled because he knew he was *not* guilty. A jury could easily believe either one.

A plus in Alston's case, not present in any of the others, was the fact that his brother had formerly worked in the city medical examiner's office. Naturally, the medical examiner had to testify as to the condition of the bodies.

When I cross-examined him, I asked; "Would you be partial to Richard Alston because you were close to his brother?"

"Oh, no," said the medical examiner.

And when he left the stand, the good doctor shook Alston's hand. Every little bit helps.

The closing speech is very important. Sometimes it can overshadow everything else that happened at the trial. After listening for weeks to conflicting testimony, repetitive testimony, technical testimony, boring testimony, a jury may well be half asleep or confused or both by the time defense and prosecution have rested.

The jurors are anxious for somebody to explain to them just what it all means. And that's what the closing speech does. It gives each side the chance to interpret all the evidence according to its point of view and to throw in stuff that can't get thrown in any other way. Lawyers quote from the Bible, recite poetry, do everything but play the violin. I cited the book *Adventures of a Young Man* by Ernest Hemingway, drawing broad parallels between the idealistic, adventurous Hemingway and the idealistic, adventurous, even foolhardy Alston. I painted a word picture of the tense summer of 1970—the summer of naked Black Panthers on the front page and "yellow dog" statements by the police chief.

"What must it have been like to be young, black, and intelligent in 1970 . . . young, black, and concerned . . . young, black, and proud."

I told the jury that the DA had deliberately taken the conspiracy indictment away from them so they could not compromise as the Conway jury had done.

Ordinarily, it is forbidden to mention the outcome of any other trial—whether another jury has acquitted or convicted can prejudice the deliberations. In this case, however, long before we'd come to closing speeches, the jury had been allowed to know the outcome of all five previous trials.

I ought to say that I had hoped to let the jury know there were two murder acquittals. Not by mentioning them, of course. I had hoped that Leonidas Brown in his testimony would mention that he'd had lunch with Conway in such and such a restaurant recently. I would hope the jury would surmise on its own that those two would not be having lunch together in public restaurants if they'd been convicted of murder one.

But as it worked out, it was Bateman who mentioned the three convictions. Stewart had just testified that he had killed Murray and Wormley but that neither Alston nor Crawford nor Tervalon nor Dowd had been with him.

Bateman: "You are saying these men didn't do it. Now you know three of those men have been convicted of murder in the first degree."

I couldn't believe what I'd heard. I really lost my composure. The DA seemed to be throwing his case out the window. In the past few years, the law has been that if a DA does something so prejudicial as to *manufacture* a mistrial, the defendant cannot be tried again.

I stood up. "Judge, I don't think I heard right."

McDermott said, "You heard right, Mr. Moldovsky."

I wasn't sure what to do next. I hate to move for a mistrial in front of a jury. It's my policy, in fact, never to do it because I think there is a definite possibility that the jury will feel you are trying to take the case away from them and get angry about it; and if the judge denies the mistrial, you are left with an angry jury. On the other hand, if I didn't move for a mistrial, I'd lose my chances to appeal that error later.

Finally, I moved for mistrial, but I mumbled it, hoping the jury wouldn't hear.

The judge had us to a sidebar conference—that is, he called both attorneys to the bench so he could talk to us out of earshot of the jury. He explained that he knew the law, he knew such a statement was never allowed, but he believed this case was unique.

The judge felt that Stewart should not be allowed to take the stand and brazenly say these men were innocent without the jury knowing that these same men had been convicted. Stewart had motive to lie, and the jury should know that. However, he added that he would permit me to bring out that Brown had been acquitted and Conway convicted only of conspiracy.

I think McDermott was truly interested in balancing the case. He really was giving both sides a chance to win.

The jury of six men and six women retired to deliberate at 5:10 P.M. and returned with a verdict—acquittal —at 8:30 P.M. Three hours and twenty minutes is not a very long time for a jury to arrive at a verdict, and during this time the jury elected a foreman, ate dinner, and, of course, voted.

I think the closing address had a major effect on this jury. It's hard to say what arguments had the strongest effect on the verdict. One woman juror told me I'd convinced her that Alston was "a nice person." I suppose she felt that a nice person couldn't have committed such terrible crimes. My gut reaction, too, is that the jurors were offended at what they saw as police callousness in this case—no policeman riding in the back of the wagon with the wounded Murray. They were offended by the cool manner of Stewart when he had admitted to murder. They were annoyed at the assistant district attorney, who had not wanted them to hear Detective Morris' evidence. The worse others looked, the better Alston looked.

I think the Alston verdict vindicated my view that the luck of the draw is as good a way as any to select a jury. One of the jurors in this case was a woman of Italian background. I'm sure Bateman thought I was crazy not to challenge her because it is common belief that the Italians of South Philadelphia do not like the blacks of North Philadelphia—and particularly not black militants. But this woman didn't treat me with any hostility, so I accepted her.

And not only did she—like every other juror—vote for acquittal, but two weeks after the Alston trial, she sent me a client who gave me $2,500 to represent him on a drug charge.

You never know.

When Alston was acquitted, Bateman took it hard. He said it showed an overabundance of the Christmas spirit. (It was true that while the jury was deliberating, the sounds of "Joy to the World" floated up from the loudspeaker in the courtyard.)

I know Bateman really felt he had a sure conviction. I know I believe Alston would have been a sure conviction if his case had been tried first. A jury trial is a roll of the dice for *both* sides.

When Stewart had taken the stand, he had said, "There is no justice."

After the jury returned its verdict, Judge McDermott turned to Alston and said, "When you perchance come upon a revolutionary, you tell him, sir, that one day in a Philadelphia courtroom you received justice."

3

Happiness Is
a "Technicality"

I'm frank to admit that whether I believe my client to
be innocent or guilty has nothing to do with how hard
I'll work in his or her defense. It may influence my strategy but not my dedication. That, of course, is part of the
American system of justice—a part that bugs a lot of
people.

I worked very hard on the case of Franklin Wallace
even though when I first got the case I was convinced he
was guilty. But by the time I was through, I had convinced myself, at least, that he was innocent. And whichever he was, I got him off.

Wallace had been accused of raping three different
women.

In the winter of 1970–71, a series of rapes took place
in a nice residential neighborhood of downtown Philadelphia. The rapes followed a similar pattern. Two or three
black kids would come up behind a young white woman
who was just about to enter her house. As soon as she

would turn the key, the boys would push her inside, force her to take off her clothes, and then take turns raping her.

Rita Prentice (not her real name), a twenty-seven-year-old nurse, came home at 9:00 P.M. one rainy night and barely noticed the kids walking past her on the sidewalk–until she found them inside the house with her.

Reporting the incident to the police later, she said, "They asked if I was alone. I don't think I answered them. They had a knife. It looked like a steak knife. Someone said to pull off my clothes and they were about to go through my purse but I was holding on to it and I was crying. They forced me onto the couch and pulled off all my clothes from my waist down. Then one guy started to pull his pants down. He got on the couch and told me to spread my legs apart. Then he decided I was not being very cooperative. He started yelling for "grease" and one of the others brought him a jar of Vaseline. Then he penetrated me and kept saying I was supposed to pump. And I remember him saying that the other guys should get ready . . . the first guy got up and another guy got on top of me. The other two were running around the house to see what they could find. When the third guy got on the couch, he told me to suck it. I said no. He said suck it or he would smash my face. I covered my face with my arms. He tried to penetrate me. Then I said my boyfriend was coming back. It just came into my head to say that.

"He started yelling to the others that I had a boyfriend coming back. They took a tape recorder and left. Then I picked up my clothes and went to the bathroom and took a bath. Then I lay down on the couch and started crying."

A police detective asked, "Did any of the males reach a climax?"

"I don't think so," said Miss Prentice.

"Did you reach a climax?"

"Absolutely not!"

(That's what rape victims love about the police . . . they ask such nice, sensitive questions.)

The detective asked Miss Prentice and three other women who reported similar events to describe their attackers. And from the descriptions, the police made up "Wanted" flyers with artists' drawings of faces. Every cop in the district got copies of the flyers.

Franklin Wallace was arrested in February 1971. According to the police, a patrolman was cruising the area where the rapes had occurred and got a call on his car radio that two black males had just attempted a strong-arm robbery (i.e., a robbery not using weapons) and were now running south on 16th Street. This patrolman then arrested Wallace and a friend and brought them to the Central Detective Division headquarters.

The police said the patrolman went back to the scene of the alleged strong-arm but didn't find a complainant. The friend was immediately let go but Wallace was detained on the grounds that he looked like one of the faces on the rape flyer.

It happens he looked like one of those faces only if you were half-blind and had a vivid imagination.

One of the drawings represented a man between twenty-two and twenty-five years of age, five feet ten inches tall, weighing about one hundred ninety pounds, with reddish-brown hair cut in an Afro. The other represented a man about the age of eighteen, five feet nine inches tall, and thin. In other words, the taller one was supposed to be older and heavier; the younger, shorter and skinnier. Franklin Wallace was fifteen years old, six feet one inch tall, weighing one hundred thirty pounds. He was younger, taller, and skinnier, and didn't have reddish-brown hair either.

Well, okay, a description isn't everything. Wallace was asked what he was doing in the neighborhood, because he didn't live there. He said he'd been to a city health center about three blocks away and was just walking around. (I later checked, and he had been at the health center an hour before his arrest.)

But obviously that answer didn't satisfy the detectives, because they continued to question Franklin Wallace, and finally the kid signed a confession. The police went to Wallace's house with a search warrant and recovered there a camera of the same make and model as one reported missing by one of the rape victims. Four victims were brought to division headquarters for a lineup and all four picked Franklin Wallace out as one of the boys involved.

I got the case of Franklin Wallace as a court appointment. Because of the seriousness of the crime, the district attorney went to the trouble of getting court permission to try Franklin Wallace as an adult rather than as a juvenile. Wallace already had a juvenile record of minor crimes—vandalism, larceny, and shoplifting. The DA was ready to go for broke on this charge.

And I have to say that when I first looked over the evidence, the whole thing looked so impossible, I figured the best thing I could do for this kid would be to bargain with the DA's office for a short sentence in return for a guilty plea. I entered into serious negotiations with the chief of major trials and the best he offered me was five to twenty years—and he was not even sure he wanted to do that. Well, maybe if he'd offered one to ten, I'd have advised the kid to throw in the sponge, but five to twenty, you might as well fight.

Fighting means reinvestigating the case from the defense point of view, starting with that report of a strong-arm robbery. I asked for the police incident report and all it said was that these two boys were picked up and turned over for investigation—nothing about a suspected strong-arm. This means that at the outset the police really didn't have any probable cause for picking Wallace up off the street. He really didn't look like either of those flyers, and if there was no robbery, he couldn't have pulled it.

It began to look like the police just arrested any black kid they saw on the general theory that the crimes were committed by black kids and if they picked up and questioned enough of them, they might damn well find the right one. Which, actually, is a theory that probably works, except that it is illegal to just haul people in off the streets willy-nilly. A lot of people who don't see anying wrong with that when it is done in a poor black neighborhood would see plenty wrong if it were done in their neighborhood—particularly if they were among those hauled in.

It's a question of degree. If you are looking for a man who has red hair and a red beard, and a patrolman spots such a man and brings him in, he might then find that he has gotten the wrong redhead with beard. But I think everybody, including the arrestee, would agree that the police have to have *some* latitude. There was, after all, some reasonable reason to be suspicious.

It's when the police want to bring in every man with a beard, or every man with a white face or a black face—then latitude becomes license.

Wallace was brought in at noon and he was held for the rape investigation. But the detective—John Chidester —who was in charge of that particular investigation was working the four-to-twelve shift that day. So Wallace just cooled it until Chidester got there.

Chidester had been working hard on this case—credit where credit is due—and he'd come up with a couple of suspects a lot more likely than my client. He had arrested, for example, one Winston Churchill Rouse, who was nineteen years old, five feet five inches tall, stocky build, with reddish-brown hair. Certainly he was a lot closer to the first composite drawing than Wallace.

Rouse had made a statement to police implicating two other young men. He said that usually he and a buddy prowled the neighborhood in question. According to Rouse, the young women they'd meet on the front steps pleaded with them to come inside and have intercourse. The gentlemen were just going around doing favors for the ladies. Now sometimes there was a third member of this little "service crew."

According to Rouse, this third young man was twenty years old. He knew him only by the nickname "Youngblood" and he knew that he belonged to the 15th and Clymer Street gang and was a runaway from the Cornwells Heights Development Center—a juvenile institution.

The police found out that Franklin Wallace was a runaway from Cornwells Heights, but nobody there had ever known him to use the name "Youngblood," it wasn't listed on any nickname record for him, he did not belong to the 15th and Clymer Street gang, and, once again, he was fifteen years old, not twenty.

But the police felt they at least had some reason to continue questioning Wallace. They asked him if he knew about the rapes and he said, yes, he did. How did he know? He said he knew Rouse, and Rouse had told him about them.

The police kept at Wallace, trying to get him to admit that, inconsistencies aside, he was "Youngblood." At 6:15 P.M., a little more than six hours after his arrest, Wallace signed a statement describing and confessing to the rapes.

One might think that he couldn't possibly describe the rapes if he hadn't participated in them. One might think he'd never confess if he weren't guilty. But experience indicates otherwise.

I studied Franklin Wallace's confession and I compared it with the confession given by Rouse a few days before. (How did I get these confessions? The district attorney is required to turn over a confession to a defense lawyer, so Wallace's confession came from the DA and Rouse's confession came from Rouse's attorney, to whom I gave a copy of Wallace's confession.)

My study indicated something very interesting. First, there was nothing material in the Wallace statement that was not contained in the Rouse statement. That could indicate that the police "coached" Wallace on what to say because they were holding Rouse's statement in their hand.

"Didn't you then ask her if she had any money? We know you did. Didn't you ask her if she had money and she said she had seven dollars in her wallet? Isn't that what happened? You say that's what happened? Let me hear you say it in your own words."

Possible. Possible.

Why confess and say what the police want you to say? Wallace told me he signed the statement because the police wouldn't leave him alone. He said they shoved him.

They scared him. Before they put him in a bare room and handcuffed him to a table, they said, "Take a good look at the street. You ain't going to see it again for a long, long time."

That wouldn't sway you? Maybe not. But it could have affected Franklin Wallace. He was fifteen, he was a kid whose I.Q. tested out at only sixty-four—he was not your average businessman about town.

So while it is entirely possible that the detectives really believed he was "Youngblood," he may well have admitted that merely to get the cops off his back.

Now we come to the lineup. The suspect is brought in and, along with a half-dozen other men who have nothing to do with the case, stands for inspection behind a one-way mirror. And the four victims are invited to come and see if they recognize any of them.

First off, the lineup was not a fair one where Franklin Wallace was concerned. Except for him, everybody in the line was between twenty-one and thirty-eight years old. He was the tallest, the thinnest, and the youngest in the line. Strictly speaking, if you are testing identity, you should have people who look roughly similar, or what's the point? There are weekly lineups conducted at prisons or youth centers where you can have your pick of match-ups. But the initial lineups are conducted at the division headquarters where the matchups are mostly policemen.

Despite the way Wallace stuck out in the line, none of the women was positive about him. Rita Prentice had been absolutely positive about Rouse and his buddy on prior occasions, but said she couldn't identify anyone for sure in this lineup.

And now the detectives did something really outrageous. This was proved later in court testimony. They gave the four women Franklin Wallace's confession to read. Then they told the women that Wallace was number four in the lineup. They also told one of the women that a camera that looked like the camera she'd had stolen was found in Wallace's house.

I might add about that camera that it was a cheap, popular brand—the kind anybody might own. There are thousands of them in the city. There was really no reason to believe that Franklin Wallace had to have stolen that camera to possess it.

The point is that this is all highly prejudicial stuff. You are asking women if they recognize somebody. Then you tell them—in a manner of speaking—that they are wrong if they *don't* recognize Franklin Wallace. So the women go back to the lineup, and, sure enough, Wallace now has a more familiar look.

Miss Prentice was a very honest woman and when I asked her at the hearing how she had been so sure the second time when she admitted she had grave doubts the first, she said, "Well, how could he have known the details of what happened in my house if he wasn't there?"

I showed her Rouse's statement. I asked her if it wasn't possible that Wallace could have been told what to say on the basis of that statement.

"Could it have happened that way?" I asked.

"I guess it could have."

"Knowing that, are you still sure that Wallace was one of the young men in your house?"

"No, I'm not sure," she admitted.

The hearing at which Miss Prentice testified was a pretrial one on the admissibility of evidence. I wanted the court to rule that the evidence the police had against my client was tainted in various ways and therefore could not be used by the DA at a trial. As soon as I found out about the detective showing the women the confessions, I went into court to get the lineup identifications thrown out as evidence. And I asked, in the same petition, for the judge to throw out the confession itself as involuntary, the arrest itself as illegal, and any in-court identifications as already prejudiced.

The judge heard testimony on the lineup identifications first. I put one of the detectives who had been present on the stand.

"Now, detective, after she told you that she wasn't sure, did you have her read this confession, which has been marked D-3, and then tell her that was the confession given by the number four man?"

"I don't recall. I may have let her read the confession. I'm not sure."

"Sir, my question is, more than letting her read it, did you also say that was the statement given by the man whom she was not positive or sure about?"

"I believe I may have told her this. I don't recall actually, counselor."

Lucky for my client, the rape victim had a better memory than the detective. Wallace said he had talked to one of the women at the lineup and told her, "Lady, take a good look at me, you're wrong."

My first victory for Franklin Wallace came when the judge suppressed the lineup identifications. But the lineup was small potatoes next to the confession. I may think the confession isn't worth the paper it's written on, but getting it legally tossed out is something else again.

The judge asked the district attorney and defense to submit briefs arguing the remaining issues of the suppression hearing.

The DA would, of course, list all the reasons why the judge should find the confession was given voluntarily. I, of course, was to list reasons why he should decide the other way.

The Fifth Amendment of the Bill of Rights in the Constitution states specifically that "no person . . . shall be compelled, in any criminal case, to be a witness against himself." That doesn't mean you can't be a witness against yourself. You can confess all over the place if you like. But you cannot be *compelled* to.

Obviously, a suspect who is slugged with a rubber hose until he admits a crime is not doing that voluntarily. And courts have long conceded that a confession given under the physical inducement of a rubber hose or brass knuckles should not be allowed in evidence.

Increasingly, in the past few years, courts have also been ruling that a confession given under what might be called "psychological duress" is just as involuntary—and illegal. What constitutes psychological duress? Long periods of questioning, for one thing.

When a court finds, for example, that the suspect had been placed in a bare room, on a hard chair, and handcuffed to a table (as was the case with Franklin Wallace), and was questioned or even just left there for six or seven hours—or fifteen hours or twenty-four hours, as has happened in various cases—and if the suspect was unhandcuffed only to eat a sandwich or go to the john—or maybe he wasn't unhandcuffed to eat or go, and wet his pants—well, maybe a confession given under those circumstances is not totally voluntary.

From the police point of view, of course, being a bunch of nice guys and sitting the suspect in an easy chair and bringing him a beer and asking if he would please mind telling them what happened . . . and would he maybe like a cigar or cigarette . . . would not bring forth many confessions.

However, the courts understand that the police do not handcuff a businessman suspected of fraud to a table for six hours and that the standards of the Constitution are supposed to apply to everyone.

The way I have been telling this story, you may wonder why I even bothered with suppression hearings. Why not just put all this incredible police activity before the jury, let them see that there really is no proof against this boy, get my acquittal, and go home?

Because I can't be sure that the jurors will see the story the same way I do. They may listen to these young rape victims tell their gruesome experiences and then be impressed by how hard, with what selfless dedication, the police have worked to find the monsters who committed such acts. They may choose to believe the confession.

And even if a victim takes the stand and isn't positive about her identification, the DA will manage to find four or five policemen who will testify that this young defendant unburdened his soul to them while they brought him sandwiches and lit his cigarettes and looked all over the city to find his relatives to tell them he was at the police station.

A jury could buy it. Who knows what a jury will do?

You could have a bunch of white jurors picturing Winston Rouse merely telling my client of the rapes—my client salivating over the lascivious details—and then wanting to hang my client just for that.

No, it is easier to try to keep a guy out of jail than to figure a way to plant a file in a cake. So if I can get the evidence suppressed, that's what I want to do.

The DA, incidentally, had not been able to get either Rouse or Rouse's buddy to identify Wallace or agree to testify against him. But while his case would have been stronger with those two as witnesses, I knew it wouldn't be lost without them either.

I definitely did not want this case to go to trial. What to do? I decided I needed more research. Half the practice of law is looking up what the law is. Every law school turns out graduates who are capable of doing excellent legal research. What they don't turn out are graduates who know how to try a case. That you have to learn for yourself—on-the-job training.

Research into the law can be very important, and in the case of Franklin Wallace—very rewarding. I do all my own research; I never trust anybody else to find what I am looking for—particularly since I'm not always sure what I am looking for until I find it.

What I found in the case of Franklin Wallace was a 1913 statutory provision applying to juveniles in Philadelphia, which in the fifty-nine years between the day it went on the books and the day I mentioned it in court, had been completely and totally ignored. No case had ever dealt with it, nobody had ever cited it. But it was the law.

The key sentence began, "Juveniles shall be brought immediately before the judge of the juvenile court . . ."

"Immediately."

Bells rang. Violins played. A heavenly chorus began to sing!

Six and a half hours isn't immediately.

Generally the law says that somebody accused of a crime must be given a hearing without "unnecessary delay" and there has been much arguing and determining

65

what constitutes delay that is "unnecessary." But the language of this old unused law was more definitive than that: immediately is *immediately*.

Apparently, the 1913 General Assembly which passed this law wanted a judge to make sure that a city kid who couldn't take care of himself was properly taken care of. The judge would make sure the parents were notified, not the police.

Why had this provision been overlooked for so long? I think because a new juvenile court law was passed in 1933 and then amended in 1939, and generally research would stop at these main bodies of law. However, I noticed a clause in the 1933 act which said that this law was not meant to repeal that 1913 provision. So I looked up the provision.

It is true that my client had been certified to stand trial as an adult, but it was also true that when arrested he had clearly been a juvenile—age fifteen. Therefore, at the time of arrest, he was certainly entitled to all the protections the law gave juveniles, even if the police didn't know what those protections were. Wallace was not taken immediately to a judge. He wasn't even taken to the Youth Study Center, which has intake facilities for juveniles, until quarter of four in the morning.

He had been arrested at noon. That had been a Friday. He did not get before a judge until Monday morning . . . this despite the fact that the juvenile court is only two blocks from the police station and the Youth Study Center is one hundred feet away.

I whipped up a brief and got it back to the judge, who then decided to suppress the confession and all identifications.

The DA's office was dumbfounded. They were going to

appeal and then they reconsidered. The courts seemed to be moving in the direction of having even adults brought immediately before a magistrate upon arrest.

So, there they were with all their evidence gone. The DA moved to *nol-pros* the case (indefinitely postpone prosecution), let it lie around for a while, and hope new evidence would appear. But I moved for trial and the judge granted that motion. It was a very short trial and Wallace was acquitted.

I wrote to Wallace's mother to be present in court to take him home; I was confident, of course, of the outcome. He had been in jail since his arrest—one year and two months! Legal maneuvering takes a lot longer to do than to read about. But his mother never showed and I gave Franklin thirty-five cents so he could take a bus home. And that was the last I saw or heard of him for a while. Then, not too long ago, I was stunned to read in the newspaper that Franklin Wallace had been arrested again on another rape charge.

Had I been wrong about him?

I find it hard to believe.

When I left court with him that day, I bumped into Detective Chidester. We talked for a while and he said to me, "No hard feelings. You've got your job to do. But I've got mine to do, too. And don't worry. We'll get him next time. He'll be back."

And he was back: he was charged with raping another woman in the same neighborhood, in the same manner —with two other boys—as the other rapes. The news story said that the woman victim had screamed and her screams had attracted a neighbor who pursued the rapists. The police then joined the pursuit and they captured Franklin Wallace.

And you know what? They kept him at detective division for twenty hours before taking him to a juvenile-court judge. Even if there was no judge sitting, they could have taken him to some administrator at the Youth Study Center to process him. If he gets a half-decent lawyer, he'll probably be out again—the same law applies.

Does this rearrest prove he was guilty all along? Maybe, maybe not. Were the police so determined to get him—because they believed him to be guilty—that they just picked him up and the real culprits got away?

Maybe Wallace was just paying another visit to the city health center. Maybe he heard a woman scream "rape" and just began to run out of sheer panic at being blamed again. Or, maybe he really was a stupid sex maniac out doing his thing.

That he would get arrested again either way is not so surprising in a big city. But it is surprising that the police would make the same damaging error of holding him in order to get a confession.

If Franklin Wallace goes free a second time, you can bet that somebody will blame it on the damn defense attorney who has no conscience and gets that son-of-a-bitch off. You can bet they'll never give a thought to the idea that the son-of-a-bitch might go free because the police did a lousy job of arresting him . . . or maybe possibly that the son-of-a-bitch didn't do it.

4

Shades of Gray

The popular stereotype of the criminal lawyer seems to be one of two extremes. He is either the crafty shyster who finagles the law in order to let thieves and murderers walk the streets unpunished or he is the fearless combination of Perry Mason and Owen Marshall who worries only about saving innocent men and women from an unfair fate.

In reality, the average criminal lawyer spends most of his time fighting for clients who are neither acquitted nor unfairly convicted. Sometimes the defense attorney has done a hell of a good job if he merely works out a deal so that the state doesn't screw up his client's life any worse than the client has already screwed it up.

As the saying goes, it isn't a matter of black and white, it's a matter of selecting your shade of gray.

Take a kid like Pebbles Finarelli. Pebbles, at the age of twenty-two, was charged with murder. And yet, from his point of view, it might be said he'd only "killed somebody with kindness." He'd helped a friend inject herself with a drug and she died of an overdose. In the milieu in which Pebbles operated, he was just being a gentleman.

Eugene "Pebbles" Finarelli was a mixed-up kid who came from a mixed-up family. He was short and skinny with hair that hung down to his shoulders and generally over one eye. His parents were separated and took out their anger at each other by fighting over the kids. I think his father was somehow on the fringe of the rackets and had been in court a couple of times himself. Pebbles' father had seen me as a DA and I guess he must have been impressed, because when I had my own practice, he hired me to defend his son.

And Pebbles gave me a lot of business: little things like fraudulent use of a credit card, receiving stolen goods, or stealing cars. And I pretty much kept him out of jail. No fancy footwork involved. For example, one can generally get a stolen-car charge dropped, when the owner gets his car back, simply by offering the car owner money in restitution.

You say, "Look, how much were your damages? Oh, a hundred and eighty dollars? Okay, I can get that for you."

The car owner would just as soon drop charges because he really doesn't want to have to take a day off from work to testify—or maybe two days if the case doesn't come up as scheduled. He's got his car back. He's had his loss made up. He's satisfied.

Pebbles was troublesome but he wasn't vicious.

One morning I came into my office and my secretary told me that Pebbles had been there, had said it was "very important," but then wouldn't wait. About an hour later, I heard Pebbles had been arrested for murder. Apparently he'd come to my office to give himself up to me, hoping I'd go with him to the police. And it does make a better impression when a fellow surrenders rather than being caught on the run. Unfortunately, Pebbles was the nervous type.

He was accused of killing sixteen-year-old Nancy Jo Winter. It had all happened at a party—a sort of party —that involved Nancy Jo, her sister Sally, fifteen, Pebbles, and a friend of Pebbles' named Eddie Kern.

Nancy Jo and Sally Winter came from a small town in the suburbs, from a staid, middle-class home. Yet they were always in trouble. They were chronic runaways; both had drug problems. In fact, Nancy Jo had just recently been discharged from a drug-treatment program in a state mental hospital.

And it was at the hospital that Nancy Jo met thirty-two-year-old Eddie Kern, who was also there to take a drug cure. Within two weeks of leaving the hospital, Nancy Jo and Eddie were shacking up.

Somehow or other, it was decided that Nancy Jo and her sister, and Eddie Kern and his pal Pebbles were all going to have a big blowout together.

They'd take a fancy room in a midtown hotel, they'd share a supply of "speed"—a drug that literally speeds up body processes, giving a feeling of power and excitement —they'd share a little sex, and they'd forget the rest of the world for a while.

So the foursome moved into Room 2009 at the Holiday Inn and they didn't come out again for two and a half days. Nancy Jo complained that she was having trouble getting high . . . she was injecting the speed and it didn't seem to be taking. And either Pebbles or Eddie or both tried to help her—maybe she wasn't hitting the vein right or something. After that, Nancy Jo got high all right. She began acting strangely, talking fast, babbling. She'd fall asleep, then wake up, babble some more, then fall asleep again. Then she stopped breathing; her heart had given out.

Eddie pulled her off the bed to the floor and tried to give her artificial respiration. Then Pebbles dragged her to the bathroom, pushed her halfway into the tub, and ran the cold shower over her, hoping that would revive her. Nothing helped.

The men got scared. Pebbles was then on probation for his past offenses. All he could think of was to get out of there. He told Sally, who was still bent over her sister and crying, that he'd call for an ambulance. Eddie Kern apparently just took off—in fact, as far as I know he hasn't been found yet.

Sally called the desk clerk of the hotel, who sent for the police and an ambulance at the same time. He went up to the room; it was a mess, bedclothes thrown around, beer cans all over. And a dead girl on the floor.

When the story broke in the papers, the impression was that these two men had lured the girls into this room, or even kidnapped them; that the two teenagers, beautiful girls with long hair and little turned-up noses, had been held captive by two drug-crazed lunatics.

Sally told the police that she didn't know the proper name of the young man who had helped her sister take that fatal injection; she had been introduced to him only as "Pebbles."

But that was enough for the police, who maintain a "nickname" file. It didn't take a lot of doing to match up the description by Sally with the right Pebbles in the police collection.

Pebbles left the hotel room at midnight. He went from there to a friend's apartment and then to a motel in another part of town.

There, as apparently was his custom, he ripped off the hotel, stealing the lamps and the TV and the bedspread for later sale to buy drugs. He left in time to pay a visit to some friends, then his parole officer, and then he came to see me.

Sadly, this case wasn't all that unique in Philadelphia at the time. Drug overdoses were becoming a very common cause of death. There were more drug overdoses in Philadelphia in 1970 than traffic fatalities! The district attorney, tuned in to public outrage, called for stiffer penalties for drug pushing. He demanded that the seller be made responsible if the buyer died of an overdose. He demanded that Pebbles Finarelli pay for the death of Nancy Jo Winter.

The DA would be out to make Pebbles look like a fiend of the worst order. And my job was obviously to counter that. What kind of girl was Nancy Jo? She was not, as some accounts would have had you believe, a sweet, demure little sixteen-year-old. She was a high school dropout who looked old enough to work as a go-go dancer in two of the toughest bust-out joints in town. Legally you have to be twenty-one to dance in—or on—a bar.

So I lined up some witnesses who could testify that Nancy Jo's morals were not the highest, that she was a sophisticated, hard-living girl. If Pebbles had been corrupting the morals of a minor, at least it wasn't a minor who looked like a minor, nor a minor whose morals hadn't been corrupted before. The case was not going to be open and shut.

The DA would have to prove that Pebbles handled the needle and injected Nancy Jo. Sally at first said only Pebbles did it, then that both men were involved.

But the first thing I did—and the most important, as it turned out—was to check on Pebbles' story that before leaving the Holiday Inn he had, as he'd promised Sally, telephoned the police for an ambulance. The DA, I knew, would make a big deal out of the fact that Pebbles had left that room, not trying to save the girl.

Through a contact at police headquarters I obtained a tape of the calls to the radio room on the night in question. Philadelphia police practice is to record automatically all calls. In case somebody faints after giving an address or something like that, the police can play back the tape to be sure they have gotten the information straight. The tapes are kept about two weeks and then destroyed, their purpose having been served.

When we came to court, the DA, as expected, painted Pebbles as a child-destroyer and played heavily on his irresponsibility in running away.

I produced a little tape cassette from my pocket and asked the judge if I might play it for him. It's a shame there were no movie cameras around to record that scene; it was dramatically satisfying, if I say so myself.

Static . . .

"Police radio, may I help you? Hello?"

A young male voice is heard stuttering, mumbling, not entirely clear . . . but clear enough.

"I [mumble, mumble] *this girl . . . Holiday Inn.* [Pause] *I think she's dead . . . think she's dead."*

"What's the address, now?"

"Thirteenth and Walnut . . . Room 2009."

74

"Thirteenth and Walnut . . . Room?"

"Twenty-oh-nine . . . Holiday Inn, Thirteenth and Walnut."

"All right . . . okay . . ."

(Click.)

I suggested that the DA consider negotiating a plea and the DA suddenly began to see it a little our way. The charge was reduced from second-degree murder, which can carry a sentence of ten to twenty years, to involuntary manslaughter, which carried a sentence of only one and a half to three years. The judge added six months to a year for drug possession.

And then, in a move that really surprised me, the judge tacked on twenty years' probation for the burglary of the motel. Usually a burglary probation is only five years.

But this was Judge James McDermott, who holds small brief for drug users. He held up a photograph of Nancy Jo Winter and said, "Now, Mr. Finarelli, I'm putting you on twenty years' probation and I'm sending you to a state correctional institution for a total of two to four years. And while you are in prison, you had better remember that when you come out, you will change your pattern of life. Because if you don't, I'm going to tear up your life into little pieces and throw it away. There [pointing] is that child. Whatever she was, she is dead. I'll wait for you to come out . . . and don't come back here again."

Finarelli came out after he'd served his minimum and he hasn't been in trouble since. I did hear from him, though. He asked me to handle the case of a friend who'd been locked up for stealing a car.

A few months after the hearing, I learned that Sally

75

Winter, the young sister, had died. She was involved in an automobile crash. An autopsy showed she was under the influence of drugs at the time.

In representing Pebbles Finarelli, I wasn't representing a boy-of-the-year who had been unjustly accused, but I wasn't representing any mad-dog killer either. He was just a mixed-up guy who had gotten himself into a real mess and my role was to convince the judge that this guy deserved a little break.

As a defense attorney, I feel that if I can get a reasonable and nominal sentence instead of a stiff one for somebody who is definitely going to get convicted, that's a win.

Not all clients understand that point of view. Clients tell me the role of a defense lawyer is to get the client off. Period. "I don't need you to advise me to plead guilty just because I did it. If I'm going to plead guilty, what the hell do I need to pay a defense lawyer for? I want off . . . I want out. . . . Think of something."

You get the client who says, "We'll fight. We'll take it to the Supreme Court," who (a) couldn't afford to take it to the Supreme Court and (b) couldn't win in any court.

My system is to explain everything that's going on to the client. I talk to him about the specific laws involved . . . about the judge's personality if I know that. I let the client make the final decision on what action we take, but I let him know all the alternatives and which alternative I think is best, first.

I level with him; I tell him what I can do and what I can't do. I give him copies of every damn paper I file, of every letter I write, of every newspaper article that appears which concerns his case. And I do that whether the client is in prison or out, is paying me directly or came to me via court appointment. I do that whether they like me or not, whether they call me a few choice obscenities, even when they try to borrow money.

And sometimes—but not always—they come around to the viewpoint that I am really on their side even when I tell them they should let me plead them guilty in return for a lower sentence rather than try to invent some miracle that is going to walk them out of court.

Take John Thomas Matthews, for example, and believe me, a lot of lawyers wouldn't want to.

Matthews did not exactly see eye to eye with lawyers. In fact, he kept firing them. Since his lawyers were all appointed and paid for by the court he did not really have the right to fire them, but he would go into court and ask that his attorney be removed and a new attorney appointed. And his old attorney would be so happy to get rid of John Thomas Matthews that he'd beg the judge to comply.

I was the last in a long list of court-appointed lawyers for John Thomas Matthews, who had robbed a finance company.

Really, it was a fluke that someone like Matthews ever got involved in a cheap heist in the first place. At the time I met him, he was thirty-one, a handsome, very welldressed man. He had been in the Air Force, had been married and divorced, and had finally decided to get a college education. He had completed one year in a college in Georgia.

Then he and a buddy named Frank Buist decided to spend the summer traveling. They drove north, carousing and gambling as they went. By the time they hit Philadelphia, they were broke. They were flat and far from home, and not too keen on admitting it by wiring for money or any other sensible solution. So they hit on this harebrained scheme to rob a finance company. At gunpoint, no less.

They marched up to a little store-front office, dressed to the nines. Matthews was carrying an attaché case and asked the nearest cashier, "May we see the manager?"

"What is it in reference to?" said the cashier.

"This is a holdup," replied Frank Buist.

Matthews told the other people in the office to go into the back room. He handed the attaché case to the cashier and told her to put everything in—and she did. Then the two men tied up the cashier and left.

Minutes later, a police officer riding in a patrol car heard on his radio that there had been a holdup. Two men had escaped in a car; one man was wearing a gold shirt and brown suit coat. The officer looked up and saw a car going around the corner containing two men—one wearing a gold shirt and brown suit coat. The officer pulled up beside the car and asked the driver to pull over. Other officers arrived on the scene, searched the car, found two handguns, one shotgun, and an attaché case containing $800.

Frank Buist saw the handwriting on the wall and pleaded guilty. He came up before a very compassionate judge who took into consideration the fact that Buist had never been in trouble before. He sentenced him to one to five years for aggravated robbery (the maximum on that is ten to twenty years) and three years' probation for burglary—that is, entering the finance company with intent to commit a crime (the maximum on that is also ten to twenty). I don't say that any judge would give a first offender ten to twenty, but five to ten wouldn't have been an unusual sentence.

Matthews didn't see it that way. He wanted to fight. I guess he just couldn't see himself in the role of a criminal; but technically speaking, that's what he was. He was drawing maps showing the location where he was arrested and the places the guns were found in the car.

I could see how he had been driving all those attorneys crazy. He could draw like Picasso but he wasn't going to get off the hook. And he didn't want to face that. He wanted to sue the police because he had clothes in the back of his car and the car was repossessed while he was in jail and the clothes were gone. I tried to explain that since he didn't have a receipt for the clothes, it would be tough to prove he had them. It went on like that.

And Matthews' case did not come up before a nice, compassionate judge; it came up before a visiting judge (a judge from another, less-populous county helping to clear up the backlog) who is known among insiders as "The Smiling Barracuda." This is a judge who leaves no doubt as to what he is going to do with this defendant as soon as the jury has finished its perfunctory function of declaring him guilty.

Matthews wanted a full trial—his day in court; he wanted to explain everything. But the outcome was never in doubt. The employees of the finance company were ready to make identification; the culprits had been caught with the guns, the money, and the tape they used to tie up the cashier. They had signed confessions. The only thing missing was a full-color movie of the scene.

We selected a jury, and I practically pleaded with Matthews that no good could come of all this. "You're going to get ten years, and don't say I didn't warn you."

Finally, he agreed to plead. I can only ascribe his change of heart to our relationship; I think he was finally convinced that I really had his interest at heart. At that point, though, I really had to sweat out a way to plead in front of a different judge. I ran upstairs to the calendar room, where Judge Edmund Spaeth was sitting. I told him we could save the cost of a trial if he would accept the plea. He would, but being a gentleman, he wouldn't do it unless the "Barracuda" (he didn't call him that, of course) agreed. The DA really didn't want a trial, so he put in a word too.

Did Matthews appreciate the way I was running around? No, probably not. Finally, we effected a compromise of sorts. Judge Spaeth accepted the plea and imposed sentence and "The Smiling Barracuda" got to give the guilty fellow a lecture "he won't forget" with the jury as an audience, after which the jury was dismissed. Judge Spaeth, happily, does not believe in giving unequal sentences for equal crimes, so he simply gave Matthews the same sentence that had been given Frank Buist, one to five years plus three years' probation.

Since Matthews had been cooling it in jail while fighting with lawyers awaiting a trial, he actually had only a few weeks left to serve before getting out on parole. Matthews had been unable to raise bail because his family was so disgraced by his behavior, they refused to speak to him, much less send cash.

In my opinion, if Matthews had not agreed to plead guilty, he would still be behind bars today. But he did get out and I heard from him, asking me to endorse him for a job with the Veterans Administration. I did, and he got the job.

Once again, this isn't the kind of guy who is innocent,

but he also isn't the kind of guy who really deserves the maximum the law allows. I think justice was done—a year in jail is enough for a witless holdup in which nobody was hurt, the money was recovered, and the lesson, I think, was learned.

Matthews hasn't referred any clients to me yet, but you never know.

5

The One That Got Away

When you deal in the criminal law, you are perform-
ing a juggling act. You are trying to protect the average
citizen against whom a crime has been committed. And
you are trying to protect the average citizen against
being imprisoned for a crime he did not commit. And you
are trying to do both at the same time.

This is one hell of a juggling act, so it should not surprise anybody to find out that sometimes all of the balls
in the air end up on the floor.

Which brings me to the case of Albie Patterson, who is
walking around today totally free and totally unsuper-
vised—something that the commonwealth fought against,
something I, as his defense attorney, certainly never asked
for, and something he sure as hell never expected.

I met Albie Patterson when he was twenty-three years
old; he'd been a firebug since the age of six or maybe
even younger.

Albie Patterson was arrested in Philadelphia when the

paper-box company where he'd been working as a stock-boy burned down. You can imagine the kind of fire a building filled with paper boxes makes. The damage was estimated at $2 million and two hundred employees were put out of work.

Nobody actually saw Albie light that fire. He was arrested because a coworker told police Albie had been the only employee with a key to the fourth-floor stockroom that night and the fire had started in that stockroom. The owner of the place said Albie had worked there for five months and this was the fourth fire to break out since his arrival.

The fire marshal was sure it was a case of arson. The fire seemed to have erupted in five locations at once; they can tell that from the areas of heaviest burning. The evidence seemed to rule out a cause like a dropped cigarette or an electrical short and to indicate something deliberate —like splashes of lighter fluid and a match. Finally, it was determined that the fourth-floor sprinkler system had been disconnected before the fire.

At the time, nobody was aware that Albie Patterson had a history of playing with matches, or even that he'd lost three previous jobs because fires seemed to happen every time Albie happened along. One of Albie's former bosses later said he'd fired the young man after eight suspicious blazes had broken out in only two and a half months. Unfailingly, it was Albie who would "discover" the fires. The boss hadn't said anything about his suspicions at the time because he knew he couldn't prove them.

Albie never had trouble finding a new job even though he'd been fired as a suspected firebug from his old. Maybe that's because Albie doesn't look like anybody's idea of a pyromaniac. He's tall, dark-haired, good-looking—the kind of kid who wears his shirt unbuttoned to the belt. He's also friendly and hard-working. Definitely not the suspicious type. Of course, it might be that Albie has no trouble finding jobs because he only seeks low-paying jobs—the kind where any warm body will do. The most money Albie ever earned that I know of was a hundred dollars a week.

When the trial on the arson charge came up—about three months after the fire—the district attorney's office wasn't ready. For one thing, the coworker who was to be the star witness was missing. He must have gone off to find himself a new job. So the DA's office asked for a continuance and then another and then another. In fact, every time the case was listed for trial, the DA managed to postpone it again. Actually, this isn't the kind of case a prosecutor relishes anyway. The evidence is all circumstantial, there's no confession, and then there is that missing witness.

I didn't represent Albie when he first got arrested. He didn't have any money, so he was assigned a lawyer from the public defender's office. After the trial was postponed for the sixth time, this public defender and the DA's office got together and agreed that the best thing to do with Albie was to have him found mentally ill and sent off to a state mental hospital.

Apparently everybody agreed with this solution, including Albie and his father. A judge then duly committed Albie, as requested by the district attorney—on a civil commitment.

I think I had better explain the difference between a civil and criminal commitment because it has an important bearing on what finally happened in Albie's case. A civil commitment is generally used for somebody who, in the opinion of his relatives or a social worker or somebody in authority, is in need of help . . . somebody unable to function in the community. That does not imply the person has done anything criminally wrong. On the other hand, a criminal commitment implies that there is good reason to believe the person has committed a crime but that he is in no mental shape to stand trial, he wouldn't be able to cooperate with his attorney for his own defense. In that case, the defendant can be sent for mental treatment and then later brought back to stand trial.

As a practical matter, it is much easier to obtain a civil commitment than a criminal commitment. All you need for a civil commitment are the signatures of a couple of doctors or the agreement of the person about to be committed.

But for a criminal commitment, you must have an extensive hearing. There must be pretty good evidence both that this person committed the crime and that he is now mentally incapable.

After all, in a freedom-loving democracy you wouldn't want those in power to be able to just ship people off to a mental hospital in order to avoid the necessity of proving charges against them.

Committing Albie civilly was "the easy way," not the proper way. Albie entered the hospital in June, presumably to stay there until the court ordered otherwise. However, by August Albie wanted out and just walked off. He wasn't found again for almost two years. He was found then only because a new man, David Vinikoor, had been appointed to head the psychiatric section in the DA's office. Vinikoor was looking through some old files and found a letter about this long-missing arsonist—a letter from the hospital director saying Albie was gone. Only *then* was a bench warrant issued for him.

Actually, Albie wasn't all that hard to find once somebody looked. After he'd left the state hospital, he managed to get married (to an eighteen-year-old who knew him for a month and obviously wasn't any more inquisitive about his past than any of his employers), and of course he got another job.

The district attorney went into court and got the arson charges reinstated. And once again, Albie was scheduled for trial. This time the prosecution managed to round up the witnesses: the fire marshal, a detective, the owner of the box company, that elusive coworker, and a company maintenance man who said Albie Patterson had shown a lot of interest in the workings of the sprinkler system.

Albie's public defender waived a jury trial, did not put Albie on the stand, and then pronounced himself "amazed" when the judge, Lisa Richette, found his client guilty as charged.

Before passing sentence, Judge Richette asked the court probation department to investigate Albie's background. Such investigations help the judge determine what kind of sentence should be passed. If the probation office research shows the defendant has never been in trouble before and has only made this one mistake, obviously the sentence would be milder than if the report discloses a police and prison record as long as the phone book.

The probation department really did a job for Judge Richette—even sending for records from another state where Albie had lived until he was fifteen. The report did not make pleasant reading.

Albie Patterson had been born to a pair of hopeless, penniless, alcoholic drifters. The family never lived a whole year at one address. When the rent was due, the family flew. Albie's father was a heavy gambler who couldn't hold a job. His mother was a neurotic who hen-pecked her husband and hated him for letting her do it. In the jargon-filled reports filed by social workers, psychologists, and psychiatrists all through Albie's childhood, his "upbringing was inadequate"; he was "rejected and abused by his parents"; and his family was "unable to establish a satisfying relationship." In plainer language, Albie Patterson never got as much attention as an ordinary dog.

But he learned how to snap back. He set fires.

At the age of seven he was found guilty of setting five fires and was sentenced to a state school for homeless boys. As one of the psychiatrists who examined little Albert phrased it, "He was *privileged* to attend the state school for homeless boys." (I have never seen a state institution yet that it would be a privilege to attend—which makes me wonder about that psychiatrist.)

There seems to be some agreement that what little Albie craved was personal attention, attention he certainly never got from his boozy family and attention he certainly wasn't going to get in a large, regimented institution.

So no sooner was Albie released from one reformatory then he would set another fire and be back at another. Albie and the psychiatrists established a mutually discouraging pattern.

One time Albie and a friend ran away from one of the reform schools and found shelter in a deserted summer cottage. Before morning Albie had burned the cottage down. His friend was so unnerved by that, he turned himself in. He hailed a police car like you'd hail a cab. Another time Albie dropped a match into a gas tank and almost roasted himself to death in the process. When

Albie was ten, a psychiatrist wrote, "He has the severe flatness and contempt for life that is reminiscent of the operators of the gas chambers and incinerators of Belsen and Buchenwald."

The psychiatrist went on to state that Albie was beyond help: "Just as with cancer and leukemia, the outlook is grim."

Yet somehow or other, none of the experts who gave Albie Patterson the once-over ever said he was totally psychotic. And so time after time Albie Patterson would be sent back to society pronounced "improved." He was said to be "compliant and cooperative," and out he'd go.

Makes you wonder whether the experts weren't just nervous about having Albie and his matches under the same roof they were under. Actually, it would make me nervous too.

When Albie was thirteen, his parents were divorced. When he was fourteen, his father moved to Philadelphia and remarried his first wife. When he was fifteen, his mother died. And that same year, when he got out of his latest reformatory, Albie moved to Philadelphia to live with his father.

As might be expected, Albie was in trouble right from the first in Philadelphia. Not necessarily arson, but the usual teenage delinquency things: disorderly conduct, street fights, stolen cars. He'd get arrested and get put on probation. Apparently nobody bothered to get his out-of-state records after those incidents. He was ordered to undergo a presentence psychiatric evaluation one time. The psychiatrist decided that Albie should be sent to a forestry camp. He wasn't, which is just as well—that would have been a great inspiration for a firebug.

Finally, six days after Albie was sent to the state mental hospital on that civil commitment, his father died. Albie wasn't yet twenty-one years old.

All of this was the past laid before Judge Richette, who had to make the decision on Albie's future. Obviously, it was a lot easier to figure out how Albie had become a danger to society than to determine what society should do about him.

Albie's lawyer was filing all the usual motions—requesting a new trial, contending the verdict was against the evidence, and the like. And then Albie himself got into the act. All those reports that had been filed on him through the years contended that Albie wasn't very smart, that he had a very low I.Q. But he wrote a letter to Judge Richette that outsmarted a lot of legal experts. Albie Patterson, on his own, asked all the right questions.

"Why," he asked, "was I given a criminal trial at all?" He pointed out that when he was originally scheduled for trial, a judge decided he was mentally ill and sent him to the hospital. What right did another judge have to reinstate the arson charge before first giving him a competency hearing? Shouldn't the court have just sent him back to the mental hospital?

Judge Richette saw that Albie had a right to have the questions answered. She asked for a three-judge panel, including herself, to provide a hearing.

She also removed the public defender as Albie's counsel because the questions Albie had raised went right to the issue of whether his attorney had done a competent job in defending his rights. I was then court appointed to represent him.

Frankly, it wasn't the greatest time for me to get a new client; I was just about to go into the hospital for a gallbladder operation. In fact, I dictated a brief on Albie's behalf from the hospital, lying down. I tossed in the entire State Mental Health Act and all the interpretations of the act. I think the thickness of the brief so shocked the district attorney, he asked for a continuance. And that suited me fine because I was able to have my gallbladder out without worrying about my client.

The brief basically argued in legal language the major point Albie himself had raised: whether or not the district attorney can whisk a person into a mental hospital on a civil commitment and then whisk him back for a criminal trial when it suits the DA to do so at a later date.

I pointed out that Pennsylvania and North Carolina are the only states in the union that permit a prosecutor to *nol-pros* (indefinitely postpone prosecution of a case) and then later change his mind and go to trial.

Most jurisdictions do not permit this because it gives the prosecutor too much latitude to abuse his power. For example, let us assume the police have arrested a man and charged him with murder. Actually, there is really no evidence against him. The prosecutor could *nol-pros* the case—which would release the man—but he would always have that charge hanging over his head. The prosecutor, instead of doing a good job of investigation, could just hope some good evidence would turn up. In most jurisdictions, the view is: once you have arrested somebody, prove the charge or drop it. There is no middle ground.

So even though Pennsylvania permits some middle ground, I argued that what had happened in Albie's case was in fact an abuse of power. I argued that by agreeing to a civil, rather than a criminal, commitment, the DA was giving up his right to further prosecution.

And I didn't just stop at the technical argument. If I'm going to defend somebody I'm going to defend all the way. And so I claimed that his original attorney had done a lousy job. And he had, too.

For one thing, the owner of that paper-box factory had testified at Albie's trial that there was only one key to the fourth-floor stockroom and that Albie had it. Yet, at a preliminary hearing, the owner had admitted that three keys existed.

Albie's counsel did not cross-examine the owner on this point. And there were several similar complaints. There were several places in the trial where the counsel could have shown that another person—maybe that coworker, for instance—could have started the fire as easily as Albie.

Just because Albie had a long history of starting fires doesn't prove he started this particular one. It could be that someone else, with a grudge against the factory owner, knew of Albie's background and used it as a cover for his own maliciousness. Could be a lot of things.

There is a lot of legal precedent that says you can't convict someone of arson just because he was at the scene of the fire and had the opportunity to start it. You have to show that no one else had an equal opportunity.

In any case, the three judges decided that Albie had not gotten a fair shake. They unanimously agreed that the commonwealth had indeed relinquished its right to seek further prosecution when it committed Albie civilly to the hospital. The judges said that the district attorney should have followed the legislatively mandated procedure.

And then they added that Albie should have a new trial.

Frankly, I didn't understand the opinion. If it was true

that the DA had relinquished his right to try Albie, why was the DA now entitled to another trial? Sometimes the law moves in mysterious ways indeed.

Nobody was happy with that, really. The DA didn't want another trial; the DA wanted the original conviction by Judge Richette to stand. The DA felt this guy was guilty, he deserved ten to twenty years in jail, and everybody should stop filing papers and send him there. The DA asked for another reconsideration of the reconsideration . . . and lost.

I offered the DA a deal: I'd plead my client guilty in return for ten years' psychiatric probation. That way he'd be getting psychiatric help although he wouldn't be confined. However, if he stepped out of line just once in those ten years, he could be tossed in jail—bang—like that!

The DA refused. The DA didn't want to have to go to trial again, but if he had to in order to make sure this arsonist was put away for ten to twenty years, then he would.

That's how it stood when we came up before Judge Curtis Carson.

I had thought the fairest thing was psychiatric probation. The DA thought the best thing to do was send Albie to jail and throw away the key. The client had started this entire legal chain of events by asking to be sent back to the mental hospital. As it turned out, all three of us were surprised.

When I stood before the judge, I did what a defense attorney is expected to do: I asked for a dismissal of the charges. I explained that if the judges *en banc* agreed that the DA had relinquished his right to try Albie and yet ordered a new trial, then it was obvious that they expected me to use the new trial to ask to have the charges dismissed. And the judge agreed. He said he did not have any other choice but to order a dismissal.

And so Albie walked out.

For all I know, with his matches in his pocket.

The DA appealed the decision but the Appellate Court upheld Judge Carson.

Albie fell through the cracks in the legal system. But this case wasn't really fought over Albert Patterson. It was really fought over the broader issue of how much power the DA can have over an individual. The DA had his chance to try Albie six times and he postponed the case each time. The DA could have committed Albie on a criminal commitment but he took the easy way, the practical way. The DA could have sought out Albie when he was first reported missing from the mental hospital, brought him to court, held a competency hearing, and then proceeded to trial.

Society may not be served by having a probable arsonist in its midst. But society is served by the system of justice that requires the district attorney to follow the rules . . . rules that protect all of us. I don't think I should have muffed my job as defense attorney just because everybody else who came in contact with Albie Patterson in his long history before the courts muffed theirs.

The case of Albie Patterson certainly put the DA's office on its good behavior. It won't pull the same kind of technical goof again . . . at least not for a while.

6

Justice Denied

Myers Douglas Thomas is now thirty years old. He has been in prison for a dozen years for a crime he did not commit. You might well ask why he is still in prison if he did not commit the crime. The answer is that once you have been caught up in the web of the law, sometimes innocence is not enough to free you.

Myers Douglas Thomas was convicted of killing seventy-six-year-old Helen Whalen by throwing her down a flight of steps.

On the evening of December 14, 1962, just a little past 5:00 P.M., a young black man came to the door of the North Philadelphia home shared by Helen Whalen, her sisters, Agnes, eighty-one, and Mary, eighty-three, and her brother, Harry, seventy-five. The Whalens were white, although the neighborhood was predominantly black. This is typical of old city neighborhoods that have changed racially: the newcomers are black and poor, only the old-timers are white and old.

"Who's there?" called Mary Whalen in answer to the knock on her door. She was expecting a boy to come help her hang some draperies.

"I am from the Gesu Church," the youth on her front step replied.

Mary Whalen opened the door. The young man jumped in, saying, "This is a holdup." He pushed Mary to the floor and shoved Agnes against the staircase. He then forced Mary to lead him upstairs to a cashbox kept in a desk. He grabbed the cashbox, tried to shove Mary down the steps, then fled out of the house. Mary ran across the street to get help. Neighbors called the police. When she returned, she saw her sister Helen lying at the foot of the stairs. Helen never regained consciousness and died in the hospital in March 1963.

In February, two months after the crime, the police arrested a sixteen-year-old named James Gilmore as a suspect in five burglaries. Gilmore claimed the police told him they were really more interested in solving the assault and robbery of Helen Whalen than the burglaries; that if he helped them solve that case, they'd drop burglary charges against him. The detectives had heard someone named "Doug" was involved . . . a tip, most probably.

Undoubtedly, the police were under great community pressure to find the young attacker of that elderly woman. Every old person in the community would live in fear until that was done. Gilmore said that when he told the police he knew nothing of the crime, they got angry at him, and told him he'd be "in jail for years." He said detectives whacked him around to help "jog his memory." (And that kind of thing does happen, even today.)

Finally Gilmore signed a statement. He said his friend, Myers Douglas Thomas, seventeen, the only boy he knew called "Doug," and another friend, Ronald Fisher, fourteen, had gone together to "get some money." Gilmore and Fisher, according to this story, waited in a nearby candy store while Thomas went into the Whalen house. Gilmore said he saw Thomas enter the home and then, ten minutes later, saw him come out. They went to a playground, where Thomas gave Gilmore and Fisher five dollars each.

The police brought in Ronald Fisher, and Gilmore repeated the story in front of him. After some additional pressure (Fisher later testified that he was beaten, "smacked in the face"), Fisher too signed a statement. In Fisher's statement, the two boys went to a candy store, stayed long enough for Gilmore to drink a Pepsi, then came out again to meet Doug. Doug gave each boy four dollars.

Thomas, who had no previous record, was arrested and charged with assault and robbery, and, when Miss Whalen died, with murder in the first degree. He was brought to trial in April 1964.

Mary Whalen took the stand for the prosecution, but her statement should have been helpful to the defense. For one thing, she said that the boy who came to her house had been there for three-quarters of an hour. Yet Gilmore's incriminating testimony said Thomas had been in and out in ten minutes. Fisher's statement to police said he'd been there only the time it took Gilmore to drink a Pepsi. And further, Mary Whalen testified in court that Myers Douglas Thomas did not look like that boy.

Question: "Can you describe him?"

Answer: "I can't. I can't."

Question: "Look around. Is that boy in the courtroom today?"

Answer: "As he sits now, I can't say. If he was to stand up, maybe I could get a better look at him." (The defendant, Thomas, was asked to stand.) "He looks thinner."

Question: "The boy who came to the house was heavier?"

Answer: "Yes."

James Gilmore testified to essentially what he had told the police in that statement. He had, of course, been kept in prison until *after* he testified—one year and three months.

But Ronald Fisher, when he took the stand, told a different story. He said that Gilmore had made up the story about Thomas, that both he and Gilmore had been afraid of the police and had been beaten into giving false statements.

Thomas' defense attorney, Robert Williams, was confident that no case had been made against his client. He couldn't be identified. Fisher's testimony counteracted Gilmore's. He didn't bother to put Thomas on the stand. And he was frankly amazed when, after long deliberation, the jury returned to convict Thomas and set the penalty at life.

After the trial, all the burglary charges against Gilmore were dropped and he was given probation as an accessory to the Whalen murder. After the trial, Ronald Fisher was convicted of perjury and sentenced to one and a half to five years in prison.

I might add that Fisher was barely sixteen years old, still a minor, when tried for perjury, yet he was tried in adult court at the district attorney's request. It is not very common for witnesses who change their testimony in court to be charged with perjury. It happens . . . but it is not common.

(If Gilmore had any thoughts about changing his testimony, presumably he would think twice about it, considering what had happened to Fisher.)

When Myers Douglas Thomas went on trial for the death of Helen Whalen, neither the prosecution nor defense mentioned the name Paul Douglas Ware. It would not have been considered relevant to the case. Yet I cannot help but feel that the events surrounding the life of nineteen-year-old Paul Douglas Ware were—and are —extremely relevant to the story of Myers Douglas Thomas.

When Thomas was in prison awaiting trial for killing an old lady by pushing her down stairs, Paul Douglas Ware was out on the street killing elderly men and women by pushing them down stairs. Although Thomas and Ware did not know each other, they lived within three blocks of each other and were only two years apart in age. Ware was four inches shorter and appeared to be heavier. (Mary Whelan said she thought the boy she'd seen had been heavier.) Both of them had the middle name Douglas and both were known as "Doug."

Paul Douglas Ware was arrested in September 1963. Mrs. Sophie Jacob, eighty-four, looked into her vestibule and saw there a young man who had struck and robbed her before. She began to scream and then called the police. Ware was caught running down the street. Ware was accused of some thirty assaults and robberies. Many elderly people were able to identify him. They told of his coming to the door, pushing his way in, hitting them, and taking money. He would knock on the door and say he was a magazine salesman or that he was from the Gesu Church. (Aha!)

Ware confessed to four murders.

One was the death of Leonard Clark, a ninety-two-year-old retired bank vice-president. On November 29, 1962, Clark opened the door to a young black boy who struck him on the face. The boy then went rummaging through the West Philadelphia house. Clark pleaded with him to stop, and told him there was nothing of value in the house. The boy then punched Clark hard. Clark was found later by a friend who came by to pick up his laundry. He died in the hospital on December 12.

Another was the death on April 22, 1962, of Daniel Gandy, eighty-seven, who had lived in the same North Philadelphia home for forty years and had operated a hemstitching business there. Mrs. Mary Gandy, eighty-six, answered the door. According to Mrs. Gandy the boy grabbed her husband and threw him down the cellar stairs, then forced her down the steps and locked her in a closet. He ransacked the house and stole a hundred dollars. Mrs. Gandy stayed in the closet for twenty-four hours until her cries were heard by neighbors who called the police. For a while, she said, she could hear her husband moaning. By the time the police arrived, he was dead.

Another was the death of Dr. James H. Kalbach, ninety-one. Dr. Kalbach had practiced dentistry from the same North Philadelphia address for sixty-five years. He charged only one dollar for an extraction. He opened the door to a young man who said he had a toothache. The young man struck Kalbach in the face, breaking his glasses. Later he turned a bedroom bureau over on top of the dentist, pinning him to the floor.

Dr. Kalbach thumped on a wall to gain a neighbor's attention. This incident occurred in May 1963. Dr. Kalbach died in the hospital in June.

And finally there was the death of Miss Florence Grauley, eighty-three, who was found in July 1963 sprawled at the foot of her basement stairs by a friend who had come to bring her a birthday cake. Florence Grauley died on the way to the hospital.

Obviously, there was a great deal of similarity in the crimes of Paul Douglas Ware and the crime of which Myers Douglas Thomas was accused. But the police never questioned Ware about the Whelan case because it was "solved." There was never a lineup in which Mary Whelan could view Ware and Thomas together.

It is surely conceivable that Ware may also have killed Miss Whelan. It is not conceivable that Thomas could have killed all the victims attributed to Ware because he was in jail when two of the four who died were attacked.

Thomas did not know that Ware existed and was in custody when he went on trial the following April as scheduled.

Ware was not brought immediately to trial. A lunacy commission determined that he was a psychotic paranoid and mentally incompetent to assist in his own defense. He was committed to the Farview State Hospital for the Criminally Insane, and there he stayed for seven years. In 1968, doctors at Farview pronounced Ware mentally fit to stand trial. However, by that time the U.S. Supreme Court handed down (in 1966) its *Miranda* decision.

Miranda said that a confession cannot be considered voluntary—and therefore used as evidence—unless the person making it was offered an attorney and warned that anything he said could be used against him. The attorney representing Ware immediately got the murder confessions suppressed because Ware had not been so warned.

The district attorney, needless to say, was appalled. The confessions could have been used if Ware had been brought to trial immediately. *Miranda* was not retroactive for those already convicted, but it did apply for those not yet brought to trial. The DA went all the way to the Supreme Court in an effort to get *Miranda* "amended" and make Ware's confessions admissible—but to no avail.

Finally, Ware was brought to trial on just one charge —the murder of Florence Grauley. Three former inmates at Farview testified that Ware had told them of pushing Miss Grauley down the steps. And the prosecution produced a fingerprint—Ware's middle left finger—found on a church envelope recovered from the Grauley living room.

Ware was convicted on June 29, 1973.

Ironically, it was just about the same time—a week before, to be precise—that I first heard from Myers Douglas Thomas. Thomas had read about me in the newspapers concerning my involvement in winning a new trial and release from prison for Lester Kibby, twenty-eight years after Kibby had been sentenced for murder (more about Kibby, which is not his real name, later). And Thomas thought I might be just the man to do something for him.

He wrote that he had a thousand dollars with which to pay a fee—he'd saved that up in over ten years of working in prison shops, sometimes for as little as twenty cents a day. He had deprived himself of any small luxury, working for the day he'd prove his innocence and go free: "I know I can win if I only am given the chance."

Naturally I went to Graterford Prison to see him and

I was impressed by his courteous, quiet manner. And also by the fact that he was a trusty there; he was so trusted he even walked me to my car to say goodbye. He was accustomed to going for weekends to a state forestry camp staying overnight in the nearby town rather than under guard.

At first I felt there was nothing I could do to help Thomas. I was not the first attorney he'd had over the years. There had not been an appeal filed immediately after his conviction; laws were different in 1964, and generally, if you couldn't afford to pay for an appeal you didn't get one. However, in 1966 Thomas was given court-appointed attorneys to take an appeal for him— two of Philadelphia's best, in fact, the late John Patrick Walsh and David Savitt, who is now a judge.

They raised legal questions on the fairness of the trial. They contended that the prosecution had not actually established how Helen Whalen had died. She was found, after all, sometime after the robber had left the house. Perhaps she had merely fallen. Perhaps her death was unrelated to the robbery.

And second, they contended that the judge in the case had given a charge that unfairly prejudiced the jury.

You'll recall that Thomas did not take the stand in his own defense. There are many reasons why a defense attorney may decide not to place a defendant on the stand. It is risky, because a jury can take umbrage at the idea that a defendant is not willing to tell his story to them personally. However, if the defendant does not take the stand, the district attorney will not get the opportunity to attack his credibility by discussing his past criminal record or some unsavory personal history.

The attorney must weigh which might influence the jury

more: a failure to take the stand or the definite knowledge that the accused has something unpleasant in his past. In Thomas' case, for instance, he had fathered an illegitimate child.

In any case, no matter what the reason why a defendant does not take the stand, it is customary for a judge, when charging the jury, to point out that the right to remain silent is a Fifth Amendment right that does not indicate guilt. However, in Thomas' case, the judge said that a defendant may choose not to testify for "any undisclosed reason." That wording, said Thomas' attorneys, coming from a trial judge, would lead a jury to believe that the defendant is really hiding something—namely guilt.

That appeal was denied. The court ruled that since Helen Whalen had no history of fainting spells, the jury was entitled to draw the conclusion that she was either pushed or otherwise affected by the robbery. And although the court voiced strong disapproval of the wording of the charge, it nevertheless said it was not a sufficient error to reverse the jury's decision.

The petition did not mention either the fact that Gilmore had lied or that Ware had committed similar crimes. But neither would ordinarily be grounds for an appeal.

Gilmore had already been called a liar at the trial; Fisher testified that Gilmore lied. But the jury didn't believe it. In the absence of any further proof to the contrary, that was that. And a court would not be impressed by the fact that another person had committed similar crimes. That alone would not prove that the convicted person had not committed the specific crime of which he was convicted.

A second postconviction petition was filed by the public defender's office in April 1968—and denied. A third petition was filed by the public defender in January 1970 —and denied.

In the latter one, Thomas' attorney took the tack that Thomas' original counsel, Robert Williams, had been incompetent. (I might add that the most competent attorneys in the world get hit with that charge. I fully expect that any of my clients, when all other appeals fail, will try that avenue. What have they got to lose?)

Williams was not specifically asked why he had not had Thomas take the stand. He was asked, however, if Thomas had ever confessed the crime to him.

If a client confesses to you, you may not report that, since the relationship between lawyer and client is confidential. But, if your client has confessed, as an officer of the court, you should not later permit him to take the stand and *deny* the crime. You may not, in short, knowingly allow perjury.

In a hearing on a lawyer's competence, the confidential relationship is waived. If Thomas had admitted the crime, Williams could have said so. But Williams said very strongly, "He always maintained his innocence. He always denied the crime. He always said that Gilmore was lying."

It seemed to me, as I pored through the meticulous files Thomas had kept on his case, that every possible avenue of appeal, including a final federal court plea, had already been tried—and denied.

I told Thomas so.

And that was when (flourish of trumpets) he showed me the affidavit: a signed statement from James Gilmore stating that he had lied!

It seems that back in 1969, a George Williams, who had been a close friend of Myers Thomas since boyhood days, ran into Gilmore in a luncheonette. Gilmore came up to Williams and asked about Thomas; he told Williams he was ashamed that he had lied. He said he'd only done it because he was afraid of going to jail; he was afraid of the police. He would do anything to help his old friend get free.

George Williams, another friend—William Tomlinson—and Gilmore then sought out Robert Williams, Thomas' original attorney, now a judge. The judge arranged for Gilmore to make a statement before a notary and told George Williams and Tomlinson to take it to an attorney. So they took it to Attorney F. Emmett Fitzpatrick (interestingly, Fitzpatrick was first assistant district attorney during the years Thomas was arrested and tried).

Fitzpatrick charged five hundred dollars to review the case, reviewed it, and said there was nothing that could be done. He wrote to Thomas that he didn't think the affidavit was of any value.

I felt differently, to put it mildly.

I felt that if we could get Gilmore to testify on the stand, Thomas really had a good chance. I felt that at least the affidavit represented new evidence, and new evidence is another reason to ask for a new trial.

We went looking for Gilmore, which wasn't too easy. Gilmore had become a wino over the years; in fact, he'd even picked up a nickname, "Winey," because of his drinking habits. He didn't even have a stable address or a stable job. (He was finally found by, of all people, my client Lester Kibby, who was interested in helping Thomas because he knew what it was like to languish in jail hoping for a new trial. And he helped himself in the bargain, because I paid him a "finder's fee.")

Anyway, Gilmore came into my office on August 28, 1973, and signed another notarized affidavit. In it he said

THE BEST DEFENSE

he couldn't understand why Thomas was still in prison, since he'd given the first affidavit back in 1969. He repeated again that he'd lied because he hadn't wanted to be charged with the burglaries. He said that after Fisher was arrested for perjury, he'd been afraid to come forward. He repeated again that he had been beaten.

He concluded, "Once you tell a lie you get deeper and deeper in. By the time of the trial for Myers Thomas, all I wanted was to get back on the street and that was why I continued to lie at his trial. As I have grown up, I have been troubled and upset knowing that because of my lies, Myers Thomas has spent years in jail. I was told he was going to get a new trial and I should not worry. Since neither of these things has happened, I have decided to give this statement of my own free will. I am prepared to testify in court or in the district attorney's office about this."

I went running right away to file for another hearing. And naturally I gave the story to the papers: an innocent man in jail because his friend had lied. Edmund Pawelec, now a judge, who had prosecuted the case in 1964, told reporters that Gilmore was his only evidence. Judge Williams told reporters he'd always believed his client was innocent. The district attorney's office announced it was launching a "full-scale investigation."

"We are as concerned as anyone that an innocent man does not spend additional time in jail," said Assistant District Attorney Edward Rendell.

Then those wonderful folks from the DA's office who are so concerned about an innocent man spending additional time in jail, those wonderful folks who told the papers they were launching a full-scale investigation, filed a petition asking that Thomas be denied a hearing.

The district attorney does not invite Gilmore to come to his office to talk to him; nope, he sends the cops to pick Gilmore up off the street. And Gilmore is hauled to police headquarters and kept on ice there for thirteen hours. And he says he's put into a little room with twenty policemen and told he's going to be arrested for perjury. He is given four lie-detector tests—count 'em, four—that the police claim are "inconclusive" (from whose point of view, I wonder). And finally, Gilmore signs a statement saying that he lied in his affidavit to me, that he'd been pressured into changing his story by threats from Thomas' friends.

And so began the "Great Affidavit War."

I was out of the office for the next few days trying a case in Pittsburgh, but Gilmore called there and talked to my partner, Larry Ring. He told Larry the police were harassing him, had cars following him. Larry got Gilmore into the office and got another notarized affidavit to that effect. (Score: three affidavits for the lawyers, one for the cops.)

Why would the police and the district attorney's office not be cooperative if there is good reason to believe an innocent man has gone to jail? Because, quite bluntly, it wouldn't look very good for them if it is proven to be so. In essence, what we are claiming is that the police phonied up a charge—pressed a kid to lie, put an innocent kid in jail—just to get an outraged community off their backs. We are charging that the district attorney pushed through a prosecution on this phony evidence. I didn't exactly think they would go out of their way to help us, but I didn't expect them to try so hard to stop us either.

I had expected them just to argue that the DA can't get excited every time somebody changes his story after

a trial; that there could be a lot of reasons why somebody
would do that.

Finally, in October 1973, we got our hearing on Gilmore's testimony and by that time Gilmore had skipped.
I put on five witnesses—witnesses to the taking of the
affidavit plus friends of Gilmore who testified that he had
told them personally that he had lied. The hearing was
continued until January 22, 1974, and the judge issued a
bench warrant for our missing witness. That meant the
police got a chance to pick him up once again.

So in January, Gilmore took the stand and said he had
lied to me and told the truth at Thomas' trial!

Aaaargh!

And Assistant DA Eddie Rendell had the incredible
gall to tell the press, "Nobody is angry at Gilmore now
that he's told the truth." (Unfortunately, Gilmore knows
only too well what can happen to him when the DA gets
"angry.")

And so the damage was done, and the judge denied our
petition for a new trial.

We were disappointed and down, but not yet out. The
circle of those who believed in Myers Thomas had at
least widened. Besides Thomas, his family, some members of the press, and me, it now included some five thousand Philadelphians who signed petitions asking that
Thomas be freed.

I naturally wanted to appeal immediately to the State
Supreme Court on the decision to deny a new trial. But
there was a hitch. Since I was a paid attorney—Thomas
had not been declared a pauper—the appeal would have
to be accompanied by a printed record of his case.

That record would include the transcript of his original trial, all the appeals, the hearings, the affidavits,

everything. It would cost thousands of dollars to print the forty copies required. This is a legal barrier that faces the average man which most people never discuss. Even if you can convince an attorney to work for free, you can still be stumped by the enormous court costs involved in an appeal.

So before I could ask the State Supreme Court for a new trial, I had to first petition to have Thomas declared a pauper so that the legal record could be forwarded as-is —just typed, rather than formally printed. That petition was granted.

But now that Thomas was officially a pauper, he no longer had the right to pick his own attorney. Another complication. The court selects a pauper's attorney and the court did not select me. But, happily, the court did select an experienced and able attorney, Joseph Bongiovanni, Jr. Joe and I got together immediately on Thomas' case. Bongiovanni filed the petition for a new trial this fall. It will be many months still before the Supreme Court acts on it . . . and many more months before a trial, if granted, could be held.

So even while all of the activity aimed at getting Thomas a new trial was underway, I was working on a plan to get Thomas out of jail on parole. If he has to wait for a new trial, it would be nicer for him to wait on the outside than on the inside.

It is not uncommon for a convict serving a life sentence for murder to be released on parole, but it is uncommon for a parole to be granted before the convict has served at least fifteen or twenty years in jail.

In order to get Thomas out sooner, he needed a commutation of his sentence.

The governor of a state not only has the power to pardon a convict entirely, he has the power to change his sentence, to give life instead of death or to shorten the term. In Pennsylvania, the governor acts on recommendations made to him by the State Pardons Board.

So Thomas requested a hearing before the Pardons Board which was granted in the summer of 1974. I was there to argue for him. So was co-author Rose DeWolf and so were a courtroom full of relatives and friends. The district attorney's office sent a representative to argue against him. The case got voluminous newspaper publicity. In the fall, the governor commuted Thomas' sentence to thirteen years to life. And that means he will be formally eligible for parole in March 1976. There is little doubt that parole will be granted.

Some have asked why we continue to try to get Thomas a new trial if he will soon, in any case, be released from jail. And the answer to that is that parole is not freedom. Parole is better than prison, but a paroled man must follow rules a free man does not have to worry about. He can't go into a bar. He can neither marry nor leave the state without his parole officer's permission.

And besides, it's natural, I think, for an innocent man to want complete and total exoneration.

Needless to say, we are well aware that we may get that trial only to have Gilmore repeat his original testimony again. But a new jury may not react to that testimony the same way again—not when they know—as they would know, that Gilmore has changed his testimony so many times, has sworn before three lawyers that he lied, has told many other individuals the same thing, and only says he "didn't lie" after long visits with the police.

Let a new jury decide with *that* knowledge in addition to Miss Whalen's testimony that Myers Thomas was "thinner" than the young man on her doorstep . . . in addition to Miss Whalen's statement that the robber was in the house forty-five minutes although Gilmore contended he was there only ten minutes . . . in addition to Fisher's testimony that the story was invented by the police.

I think you can't help but wonder whether that jury back in 1964 would have come to the conclusion it did if it had known that Gilmore would later be rewarded for his testimony and Fisher punished for his; if it had known that Paul Douglas Ware, a young man from the same neighborhood, would in a very short time be accused of four murders and some thirty assaults on elderly people. I tend to think these things might well have raised reasonable doubt in the jury's collective mind about Thomas' guilt.

Reasonable doubt, of course, is what it is all about. I cannot prove conclusively that Thomas is innocent. His mother, Mildred Thomas, says that at the time of the incident at the Whalen house, her son was at home. But a mother's word is not the strongest alibi.

The question, however, is not whether Myers Douglas Thomas can prove himself innocent, but whether the prosecution can prove him guilty beyond a reasonable doubt. The jury in 1964 seemed to have no such doubt. I think they didn't know the whole story.

We often hear the phrase "Rather ninety-nine guilty men go free than one innocent man go to jail." Somehow or other, that has not applied to Myers Douglas Thomas.

7

Justice Delayed

Obviously, I believe a defendant's fate often hinges as much on the competence of his attorney as on what he did—or didn't do—and that a lot of men and women are either in jail, or in jail too long, just because they didn't have really top-notch, dedicated counsel.

It happens that a lot of men and women who are in jail feel the same way—which is why the study of law is so popular there. The "jailhouse lawyers" give their own cases the kind of meticulous attention and care that few paid lawyers can afford to devote to them. And some of them really do a damn good job.

Like Lester Kibby.

Kibby had been involved in a teenage gang killing in 1944. You hear so much about gang warfare in the cities today, that you tend to forget what an old phenomenon gangs really are. There have been teenage gangs, both black and white, in poor urban neighborhoods for generations.

In 1944 two of the best-known gangs in Philadelphia were the Tops and the Bottoms. The Tops operated north of a major shopping street called Lancaster Avenue; the Bottoms operated south of it. Lester Kibby, then sixteen years old, was a member of the Tops.

The Tops were in a mood for a rumble with the Bottoms over the usual real or imagined mistreatment of a member and, on this October day, moved into Bottoms' turf to confront the gang at an ice cream parlor.

A group of Bottoms were actually sitting over plates of ice cream in a booth when the Tops arrived. There was some pushing and shoving and general milling around. The Tops went in and out of the store.

Somehow or other in this general melee, there was a confrontation between seventeen-year-old Fairbanks Caldwell and Lester Kibby. Caldwell said something to Kibby and Kibby went after Caldwell, grabbing him from the booth. Caldwell kicked him. A buddy handed Kibby a revolver. Kibby aimed the gun into the air and pulled the trigger; it clicked. He pointed it into the air a second time, and pulled the trigger again—another click. Then he aimed it at Caldwell, who at that point started to run away. He squeezed the trigger and the gun went off.

"I'm shot," Caldwell said, and fell.

Kibby was arrested and the boys from the Bottoms gang, who naturally had no love for him, said he had pointed the gun at Caldwell, not into the air, and had fired it three times until Caldwell finally fell.

Kibby always claimed that when the gun clicked twice, he figured it was inoperable and he was only trying to scare Caldwell when he finally aimed the gun at him.

On January 11, 1945, Kibby appeared before a three-judge court—all the members of which are now dead—

with an attorney, also deceased, whom I will call Charlie Farnsworth rather than identify him at this late date.

Kibby pleaded guilty to murder generally, which meant it was then up to the panel of judges to determine whether that should mean (a) first degree, (b) second degree, or (c) voluntary manslaughter. Or to put it another way, the judges were to decide whether, when taking that gun in hand, Kibby had acted (a) with a specific intent to kill Caldwell, (b) with wanton recklessness and hardness of heart, but not specific intent, or (c) with some serious provocation.

Kibby claimed his attorney had said to him, "You're just a kid, plead guilty and the worst you'll get is second degree. That means you'll be sent to Camp Hill (which is a prison for juveniles), and you'll be out by the time you are twenty-one." He took his attorney's advice and pleaded guilty. The court then decided it was a first-degree murder and sentenced him to an adult prison for life.

In 1961, when he had served more than seventeen years, his sentence was commuted from life to sixteen years and nine months and he was paroled on a lifetime parole. Two years later he was back in jail on a technical parole violation: keeping company with other ex-cons, bad companions. Kibby complained that if you are in jail for seventeen years, the only people you know are people from jail—but back he went.

In 1966 he was paroled again. In 1969 he was back again, this time with a robbery charge over his head. Kibby had no excuse for that one—he'd just messed up. He got a three-to-six-year sentence, which he was to serve whenever his parole on murder came up again.

Kibby's tastes of freedom had been short but sweet and he immediately hit the lawbooks to look for a way to reach freedom once again. In his long term in prison,

Lester Kibby had become a jailhouse lawyer. He was, when I met him, the chief assistant in the paraprofessional legal-aid clinic at Huntingdon Prison ("a concerned residents' legal project to assist prisoners").

Kibby was not only working on his own case, but on the cases of dozens of other prisoners who did not have the funds to hire a regular lawyer. These men all knew that if they didn't file a paper for themselves, no paper would ever get filed. (This, of course, is not a problem a well-connected criminal from a well-heeled family or organization must face.)

The jailhouse lawyer has among his "clients" prisoners who cannot read or write, who don't know there are appellate courts or federal courts, who don't know they are entitled, under the statute, to a copy of the notes of testimony, etc., etc. If it were not for the jailhouse lawyers, these men would never get any help at all. And there is a practice in prison that while a fellow prisoner cannot charge money for his advice, he can accept a carton of cigarettes or a book or candy as a gift. In some prisons, there are going rates for a habeas corpus petition or other kinds of petitions. And besides these "gifts," the jailhouse lawyer has a certain status and prestige among his peers, which doesn't hurt either.

The most common kind of petition a prisoner files is a postconviction motion—that's an almost automatic request for a new trial. Some years back, I helped work out a standard form for filing postconviction motions that makes life easier for both prisoners and judge. Instead of receiving a hundred pages of illegible handwriting arguing all kinds of mumbo-jumbo, the judge now receives a six-page mimeographed form on which one or all of the standard complaints have been checked off.

The standard complaints are such things as: "I didn't

have an effective lawyer"; "I didn't mean to plead guilty"; "I didn't have the right of appeal"; "I was denied the right of confrontation"; and so on.

Lester Kibby, who had helped many other men win new hearings, attempted to win one for himself. He attacked his original conviction and sentence, contending that his plea of guilty was unlawfully induced by a confession given only after illegal pressure and beatings. He said he was denied counsel not only when he gave that confession but also at his preliminary hearing. And he said he was ineffectively represented by counsel at his trial.

A postconviction hearing was held for Kibby in October 1969 and the judge denied him relief. Kibby appealed that decision to the State Supreme Court, but it was upheld. Then, all on his own, Kibby filed for a new trial in the federal court, arguing that he had been denied his right of appeal in 1944 when he was sixteen. His lawyer had not appealed his case. No one had appointed any other lawyer for him, and therefore he had lost his chance to appeal at that time.

What he won from the federal court, then, was the right to review the entire proceedings—as if it were 1944 again. Everything that had happened back then became fair game.

Without going on like a textbook on law, let me just say that it was pretty tricky legal maneuvering for Kibby to know how to file that particular federal petition. And in filing it, he proved that the old saw "A man who is his own lawyer has a fool for a client" is not always so.

Once he had won the right to appeal "now as then," the president judge of our court appointed me to represent Kibby in that and all subsequent appeals. The court recognizes that an amateur may do very well, but he is still an amateur.

So I wrote to Kibby to see if he could arrange with prison authorities at Huntingdon, which is about three hundred miles from Philadelphia, to transfer him to Graterford Prison, which is only thirty or forty miles, to make it easier for me to confer with him. And he wrote that he was planning to come home to Philadelphia on furlough during the first week in July and he'd drop by my office.

That was how I found out that Lester Kibby was probably the most trusted trusty at Huntingdon . . . a regular first citizen of the place. He worked outside the gates and got a week or so off once in a while. He may have made some mistakes when he got on the outside, but the people on the inside who knew him best thought he was the greatest.

We reviewed together the way Charlie Farnsworth had handled Kibby's case. And in my opinion, Farnsworth did a lousy job. I don't mean he was an evil guy or anything. Actually, he had taken on the case for charity. Kibby's mother had pleaded with him to help and told him she couldn't pay anything.

Farnsworth had visited the kid *once* for fifteen or twenty minutes while visiting other prisoners awaiting trial. There is nothing wrong in seeing him along with others; we all see a lot of people one after the other when we visit a prison, because you can't run back and forth to a prison every day. But Farnsworth only saw Kibby that once and never again until he walked into court. You have to wonder how well prepared he could have been.

He never bothered to challenge the way Kibby had been treated after he was taken into custody. And there had been plenty to challenge.

Kibby had been kept incommunicado for a number of days. He was taken from one police station to another. His mother kept following him around, but she was never allowed to see or talk to him. This wasn't an uncommon practice, really. Often it would be done because the police wanted to clear up crimes at various detective divisions . . . and they hauled a suspect from division to division because that's where the files and the witnesses were. The suspect would be put in a lineup at one police district and then taken to another for a second lineup there. Today that's illegal, but I wouldn't be surprised to hear it still happens on occasion.

When I was still in the DA's office, we had one man in custody who we were sure was involved in some burglary capers. And we were moving him around while his lawyer was calling every ten minutes to protest. At one point we had him in one office while I was in another office talking to his lawyer. "Where is my client?" the lawyer screamed. "Do I look like a policeman?" I screamed back. He left. I hadn't actually lied.

Anyway, back in 1944, this boy was taken from police station to police station for four days before he signed a confession and he wasn't brought before a judge for two weeks. And that kind of delay was illegal. It's illegal now and it was illegal then.

I went up to the dusty, cluttered rooms on the eighth and ninth floors of Philadelphia's City Hall where old court records are kept and found the file of the old indictment and docket entries, both of which played a part in our appeal. I also got the transcript of the first trial. I'm happy I don't often have to look for records that are twenty-seven years old—what a mess.

According to the old transcript, Farnsworth opened the

trial by saying; "If your honors please, we will plead guilty to second-degree murder, sirs."

The court replied, "You are here on a general plea. You have already pleaded."

Farnsworth: "We plead guilty, sirs; I submit the crime has not risen any higher than second degree. . . ." And then he must have gotten a mean look from one of the judges because he went on to say, "I withdraw the statement. And if the court will receive my recommendation, I'll proceed to show what type of boy the defendant is without going on the merits of the case."

Remember that while this is going on, Kibby is only sixteen years old, is not a lawyer, has not studied law, and doesn't know what the hell is going on. He doesn't know that a plea to murder generally can be accepted by the court as first as well as second degree. Kibby contends the lawyer told him it would be second degree—and the lawyer's remarks in court seem to bear this out.

Furthermore, Kibby's signature does not appear on the old bill of indictment. Usually, if a person pleads guilty, he signs on the bill of indictment that he pleads guilty. The lawyer had signed but the kid hadn't. That seemed to me further proof that the kid was relying entirely on the lawyer and that the lawyer hadn't told him everything.

Beyond that, I studied the record and was appalled at the amount of hearsay evidence that went into it. Other members of the Tops gang gave statements that were read into the record. Those statements were bound to be self-serving because those kids didn't want to be charged as accomplices and share the blame. So naturally they gave statements about how "shocked and amazed" they were to see a gun in Kibby's hand. One of those statements helped to make the case for first-degree murder. One boy claimed Kibby had pointed the gun and said, "I'm going to kill you."

If you tell somebody what you are going to do before you do it, it does indicate premeditation—specific intent.

Farnsworth did object to this testimony and to the fact that the witnesses were not present for cross-examination. But he was overruled.

In fact, the law back in the 1940s permitted that ruling. When Kibby was first arrested, police brought certain gang members in to repeat charges in front of him. He didn't say anything (he may well have been afraid to say anything, surrounded as he was by policemen). But in those days, the fact that the charges were made in front of him was considered sufficient to meet the constitutional requirement that an accused be allowed to confront his accusers. Today, of course, that confrontation must take place in a court of law.

Something else permitted back in the forties that was later declared unconstitutional was the so-called "tacit admission rule." This meant that if somebody accused you of something and you didn't deny it, you had tacitly admitted it. Thus, not only were the charges of the gang members admitted into evidence at Kibby's hearing, but his failure to reply to those charges at the time were admitted into testimony as if they were admissions of guilt.

And if all this were not enough going against sixteen-year-old Lester Kibby, a strange thing happened at the end of the trial. Farnsworth put Kibby's mother on the stand to get the usual character testimony: this is a nice kid, he's good to his mother, etc. But one of the judges said cynically of the mother, "She will say that he's a good boy, that she never knew him to be arrested and never had any trouble with him."

Mrs. Kibby then said, "Oh, I can't say anything like that because he has been arrested for sneaking into the movies without paying."

Thus Kibby never actually had a character witness speaking for him. Yet, though the defense had not been able to show good reputation, the prosecution went right ahead putting on its witnesses to show Kibby had a bad reputation at his school. And that was wrong. The court should not have permitted it. If the defense doesn't show the defendant as a good guy, the prosecution should not get a chance to show he's a bad one. That's the rule.

So when I got my chance to argue for Kibby, twenty-seven years after the fact, I argued that the court had been prejudicial. At the time, one of the judges who had been on that original panel was still alive and was now serving on the appeal panel. And he was a judge who had been a professor of mine in law school, a judge I highly respected and one who had helped sponsor my career. I admitted I didn't really like arguing that he'd been wrong so many years before, but he merely said, "Go ahead, Joel."

I went ahead. I argued that Kibby hadn't had effective counsel, that he hadn't known what he was agreeing to, that he should have gotten a speedy arraignment, and that the confession had been involuntary—and that if one of these was not sufficient to warrant a new trial, the combination of them all should be. The court agreed.

Kibby could have demanded that new trial and he would, I'm sure, have been acquitted. You can imagine the difficulty the DA would have trying to round up witnesses to a twenty-seven-year-old crime. And this time, Kibby would have had to be tried by 1973 rules—cross-examination of witnesses and all.

However, a trial would take a while. And at that point Kibby had already served more than twenty years, which was the maximum for murder in the second degree. He was anxious to just get out. So he agreed to plead guilty to murder in the second degree, this time fully understanding what he was doing. He was sentenced to ten to twenty and immediately discharged from that sentence. Of course, he still had that three-to-six-year sentence on robbery to serve, but the DA agreed to credit all the time he'd served in excess of twenty to that sentence and parole him for the rest. So no matter how you looked at it, Kibby was out.

Kibby told the court, "I want to thank you gentlemen for recognizing my rights. I hope I will show you you didn't make a bad decision."

A hell of a guy, Lester Kibby. I may have been helpful in piloting that appeal for a new trial, but the fact remains that he would never have had the chance to make that appeal had he not filed his own petition in federal court. If Kibby hadn't been a jailhouse lawyer he would never have gotten me or anybody as his court-appointed lawyer.

People like Lester Kibby make you stop and think. When he was sixteen, he was a member of a gang, he had dropped out of school and taken a job in the Philadelphia navy yard. Like a lot of poor kids, it probably never occurred to him that he had brains and that he could do a lot with his life.

If he'd been born in a different neighborhood, if he'd

had some other opportunities, he might be giving me competition for clients today.

Kibby still does legal work for men he knew in prison. They send him questions and he gives out advice and fills out forms, follows up on appeals, and writes petitions for them.

But he works full-time as an upholsterer. He didn't tell the boss he'd been in jail when he applied for the job. He told him he had been working for an uncle who had a storage company. The uncle didn't have a job for him but agreed to be a reference.

He says he doesn't worry that his boss will find out now that he's an ex-con. He says he figures now that he has proved he can do the job, it won't matter. The problem for ex-cons, he says, is just getting the job in the first place.

I once mentioned to Lester Kibby that it was a shame nobody had recognized his potential before he'd gotten into trouble at age sixteen. Maybe then Caldwell would still be alive and Kibby wouldn't have spent the best years of his life—between sixteen and forty-five—in prison.

He just smiled sadly. "I never thought about reading much until my back was to the wall."

Not long ago, I heard that Kibby got hit by a taxi while crossing the street. His leg was broken and he was laid up for six weeks.

A hell of a civil suit there. But you know what? He didn't bring the case to my firm. He took it to some total stranger! How about that? These jailhouse lawyers think they know it all.

8

A Performance

Many of the strategies I use as a defense attorney I learned from Cecil Moore, a tall, cigar-puffing black man who is probably the most famous—certainly the most flamboyant—attorney in Philadelphia. Cecil is a legend in his own time for the way he can age a case, stretch out a trial, and generally make the district attorney wish he had never heard of either Cecil or his client.

If Cecil Moore is on the case, the DA can throw out all his plans for cutting costs and reducing the backlog. Cecil can find more ways to get a trial postponed than a confirmed bachelor for avoiding his wedding day. Either Moore is already involved in another case when the DA would like to schedule a trial, or he has a defense witness who is missing, or he objects that one of the DA's prosecution witnesses is missing, or any one of a thousand other reasons.

And while the case is dragging on, Moore's clients fondly hope that the prosecution witnesses will grow old and die, or get hit by a truck, or get discouraged at always showing up in court and being sent home again, or forget whatever it was they planned to say.

Moore didn't invent this practice, you understand; he has merely raised it to a fine art. Philadelphia court officials have occasionally tried to outfox Moore by assigning one judge and one assistant district attorney to do nothing else for six months except handle Cecil Moore cases. That way, Moore can't plead he has to be in another courtroom on another case when a case he has been aging for a while is scheduled to begin. The only problem with that idea is that after the stated period of time, both the judge and the DA are ready for a mental hospital while Cecil is rarin' to go on.

Because when Cecil finally goes to trial, he really makes a trial of it. Like another Cecil—Cecil B. De Mille—Cecil Moore is known for his "casts of thousands." Cecil will call everybody possible as a witness. He will call prosecution witnesses that the prosecution didn't call. If there were twenty policemen on a murder scene or thirty firemen at a fire, he will call every one of them to ask a question, even though most of them did not actually do any investigating. Cecil will demand to see the report each of these men on the scene turned in. And of course most of them didn't turn in any report. And Cecil will be "astounded." There is no report? The report is missing? Ah-ha. What are they hiding that they didn't have this man put in a report?

Cecil will harass the prosecutor and start fights with him—nothing that will anger the judge unduly for the most part—but just enough to get the DA flustered in front of the jury. He'll move for a mistrial every ten minutes because of a DA's question or a DA's remark, trying to convince the jury that the power of the state, all those policemen, the entire system, is arrayed against this poor defendant, and all the defendant has going for him is Cecil Moore and his big mouth.

And frankly, sometimes the only thing some of Cecil Moore's clients *do* have going for them is Cecil's mouth.

Cecil believes in creating conflict within a jury—any kind of conflict. Black against white, female against male, single against married, young against old, possibly liberal against conservative. If you can get opposing types on the jury, it might result in a hung jury, one that cannot possibly agree. And that's good for the defense—second best to an acquittal. And a split jury will sometimes result in an acquittal, because if six or seven have reasonable doubt, there's a good chance the others will buckle in and go along. Of course, if ten are for conviction, it may go the other way.

It may be that a jury will get angry at Cecil Moore for the way he is always snapping and snarling at the DA or a witness, or at the way he stretches out a trial.

But that won't necessarily hurt Cecil's client. The client will be sitting quietly at the defense table, dejected and dignified. His demeanor will be in sharp contrast to that of his flamboyant counsel. The jury could say: should we blame him for the behavior of his lawyer? Look, even he seems embarrassed by it.

I know the dread that facing Cecil Moore engenders in the heart of a mild-mannered DA, because when I was in the DA's office I had to face him. Cecil and I squared off in the case of Willard Cockfield, who in my opinion had murdered three people—including two small children—and deserved every effort the commonwealth could make to put him away.

Cockfield had been convicted of arson-murder back in

1964—after fourteen Moore-arranged postponements and a nine-week trial—of the 1960 murder of Ida Quattlebaum, thirty-two, and her two children, Bernadette, ten, and Stephanie, six. Cockfield, then thirty-seven, had been dating Ida, who was separated from her husband. Then they quarreled and she told him she didn't want to see him any more. Angered, Cockfield went to the house one night while its occupants were asleep, spread gasoline around, ignited it, and then watched as the place went up in flames. The entire upstairs was gutted. It was an old row house and the fire spread quickly. Ida Quattlebaum died in bed. The two little girls had apparently tried to reach a window and were heard screaming before the flames reached them.

Neighbors tried to rescue them but were forced back by the heat. In the photographs that the fire department took after the fire had burned out, you could see where the body of one of the girls had imprinted itself—had become fastened—to the plaster. It was a gruesome crime.

The police naturally went looking for the rejected suitor, Cockfield. They brought both him and his automobile to headquarters for further investigation. While going through the trunk of the car, they found an empty two-gallon gasoline can and a charred role of toilet tissue. Cockfield explained that by saying he had poured a little gasoline on Mrs. Quattlebaum's front porch, but he hadn't touched a match to it.

The jury—despite all the side show I am certain Moore presented—apparently took this admission plus the evidence of the can and the toilet tissue and decided that Cockfield was guilty.

Moore, naturally, appealed the decision. And a couple of years went by as posttrial motions were filed, the record was transcribed, the brief was prepared, etc. And during this time, the Supreme Court handed down the decision known as *Mapp vs. Ohio,* which bars unreasonable searches and seizures. It pretty much meant that the police had to have a warrant and a good notion of what they were looking for before they could search a home or car. The strictures of *Mapp* have been relaxed in later court decisions, but in 1966 they were held to apply in the case of Willard Cockfield.

The police had gone through his trunk without a warrant the *day after* the car was taken into custody and left parked on a police lot. That meant the gasoline can and charred toilet paper were illegally obtained and could not be used as evidence. And since Moore had challenged the legality of that evidence before the 1964 trial, Cockfield was entitled to a new trial.

That trial was held in 1969. As prosecutor, I had to face the fact that my best evidence was now gone. And it was pretty obvious that Cockfield was not going to be convicted a second time unless some new evidence was developed. So nine years after the crime, we reinvestgated it.

The police and district attorney's detectives went door to door in the Quattlebaum neighborhood to once again ask if anyone remembered seeing anything or hearing anything that would be helpful.

We still had that partial confession of Cockfield's that he had poured gas on the porch, but we had no corroboration of that. And Cecil Moore, knowing perfectly well that we would not be allowed to bring forth the gas can and tissue, would be screaming, "Where's your corroboration? Show me, show the jury one piece of evidence that says the police didn't put those words in my client's mouth. Show me a gasoline can. Show me anything."

The detectives did find one elderly man who said he saw Cockfield on the street at the time of the fire. He recognized him as the man he'd frequently seen with Mrs. Quattlebaum. But he was frank to say that he would not testify. He would go to jail first. He wasn't going to take any chance that this revengeful nut would go free and then come burn down his house with him in it. That reinforced our belief that we had the right guy —but it didn't help the case.

The defense actually had a strong positive bit of evidence to put before the jury. The police had done tests on the clothing Cockfield wore the night of the fire and did not find either gasoline stains or scorch marks on any of it. Moore would naturally make a big thing out of that. If this man had set a huge gasoline fire, how come the fire had never touched him?

In addition, the fire did not burn the porch—where Cockfield had admitted pouring gas—it burned the stairwell leading to the second floor, which was located a good fifteen feet inside the front door, and, of course, the second floor itself. We would have to show that Cockfield had been inside the house, not just on the porch. But if he was inside the house—once again—how come he didn't get burned?

When the files on the Cockfield case were turned over to me, along with them came a small box containing pieces of would-be evidence left over from the first investigation in 1960. Happily, the DA's office never throws anything away, even if it is not used in a trial. And twenty years after a crime, you can find old bullet casings or hair samples peacefully waiting on a shelf, just in case they should be needed.

In this box was a paper bag containing some keys on a

key holder, a photograph, and some other mementos of the deceased Ida Quattlebaum. The mementos indicated that Ida had some sisters with whom she was very close. So I went to talk to those sisters. I showed them the key case, the photo, and the mementos and asked if these jogged their memories in any way.

One of the sisters told me that when Mrs. Quattlebaum and Willard Cockfield were lovers, Cockfield was given a key to the house. But after the quarrel, Ida took the key back and put it in that key case—which was her holder for extra keys. The day before the fatal fire, this sister had visited Ida and claimed Ida said to her, "I heard a noise in the house last night. And this morning I looked and my spare key to the front door is missing."

That could explain how Cockfield might have gotten inside the house on the night of the fire without breaking either the lock or the door. The sister also told me that two or three weeks before the fatal fire, Mrs. Quattlebaum and Cockfield had a fight and Cockfield had set fire to the back porch.

Mrs. Quattlebaum had called the fire department— there was a record of that—but unfortunately she did not say the fire had been deliberately set. The firemen just put it out and went away.

I thought the sister would make a good witness, but I could picture what Cecil Moore would say once she'd taken the stand: "How desperate the DA must be to pull in these relatives to frame the poor defendant." One thing you can always be sure of with Cecil. He never does things by halves. He will attempt to chop every witness, not just in two, but into lots of tiny pieces. He shouts. He screams. He challenges. He objects. He staggers around and makes the jury nervous.

Two women on the Cockfield jury became so upset by Cecil's performance that a doctor was brought in to examine them. He declared they were suffering from "acute antipathy" to the defense counsel and couldn't function! When a jury is picked, there are always fourteen jurors selected even though only twelve will actually vote on the verdict. That is done in case a juror or two becomes ill. For five weeks, we sat with only twelve jurors and if any of those had gotten sick, there would have been a mistrial.

Moore, of course, continually insulted me—nothing personal, he insults every DA he comes up against. He called me a draft dodger and a little boy. And under his breath he added cocksucker and faggot. The latter was inaudible to the judge but just loud enough for the jury. I didn't just lie down and take it, of course. I fought back.

At one point, I accused Cecil of being drunk and asked the judge to hold him in contempt of court. So the Cockfield trial was recessed for an hour to make time for a contempt trial for Cecil. And Cecil brought in his own attorney to defend him. He was acquitted. Let me tell you, all of this is more wearing on the DA than on Cecil. He thrives on it.

I held a press conference after one session and piously announced, "I will not be sidetracked, insulted, or cursed by Mr. Moore without taking the appropriate action to uphold the dignity of this court [etc., etc.]."

The reporters rushed to Moore for his response, and waving his ever-present fat cigar, he said, "I'll be socking it to him right down the line."

That's Cecil.

When one of my police witnesses takes the stand, the first question Moore asks on cross-examination is whether he has gone over his testimony with me—the DA—before taking the stand.

Well of course he has. I always meet with each witness and go over what they are going to be asked and what I think they might be asked on cross-examination. This is done by both sides in any trial. There is no other way to do things, because a jury trial is a battleground in which the lawyers are trying to create an illusion or humiliate or embarrass or force a witness to say something he or she doesn't want to say.

Cecil is a master at this and if you want to combat him, you have to prepare a witness for the ordeal he is going to face. It's only humane.

But Cecil, of course, makes the most of it. He calls it a "dress rehearsal." He tries to convince the jury that I've cooked up this evidence and planted it with my witnesses. He wants them to think it's all phony.

"Ladies and gentleman of the jury, is the DA trying to get perjury and false evidence to convict my client?

"Detective Smith, isn't it true that the DA has told you to say just what he wants you to say?"

I jump up and object, and the judge sustains me. But Moore will just go back and ask the same question again. And the judge will sustain me again.

And then Moore will do it again. And I'll ask the judge to cite him for contempt or else the judge will tell him to shut up and get on with the case. And then Moore will say my remarks about him have prejudiced the jury and he will demand a mistrial.

Help!

From the first, despite the jockeying on both sides, I was aware that I would never get a conviction for Willard Cockfield if I did not show that he could have started that fire and not gotten gasoline stains or scorch marks on his clothes. That was the nitty-gritty. Moore was making me out to be an evidence inventor. I was passing around gruesome photographs to make the jury sick.

But the important issue was: Could he have started that fire or not? Even if he did have the key . . . even if he could have easily and quietly sneaked into the house and poured gasoline over the staircase, how could he have set two gallons of gas afire with gas vapor all around and not show any signs of it on his clothes?

The credit for answering that question goes to fire department Lieutenant Edward Aleszcyk. Aleszcyk said that if gasoline were poured on the steps, gas fumes would float through the air toward the air space under the front door. If somebody put a lighted cigarette into a pack of matches and left that on the porch, the fumes would eventually reach the matches and the cigarette would eventually ignite the matches. And that would ignite a fire. The fire would then be carried back into the house across all the fumes, to the steps, then up the steps to the second floor.

Because of the obvious delay in allowing the fumes time to drift under the door and the cigarette time to burn down to the matches, the person who set the fire could actually be far away from the fire when it started, and therefore not have any stains or scorches on his clothing.

It was a theory well worth testing. The firemen built a model of a staircase, small enough to be brought into a courtroom. Moore naturally objected to it, so we had to give our demonstration three times in front of the judge alone before he would permit the jury to view it.

The firemen saturated a sponge with gasoline and set it at the top of the stairs. They placed a hollow tube down the steps. Then they struck a match at the bottom of the tube. The flames swiftly shot through the tube— which by then was filled with gas vapors—to the sponge and set it afire.

The jury could see for itself that if you ignite vapors, the flames travel back in the direction from which the vapors came.

We had testimony from Lieutenant Aleszcyk about wind currents and drafts and all of that. Moore shouted that there was a "liar" in the courtroom . . . looking meaningfully at Aleszcyk. I said there certainly was a "liar" but he wasn't on the stand, and looked meaningfully at Moore.

This trial lasted seven and a half weeks, including sessions that ran as late as 11:00 P.M. because the judge was determined not to permit Cecil to tie up the courtroom forever. I called thirty-two witnesses. Moore called twenty-three. The jury was out seven hours and came back with a guilty verdict.

The judge, Robert N. C. Nix, Jr., told the jury he thought the verdict was most "appropriate." Nix doesn't usually say that kind of thing. He added that there was no doubt that Cockfield was guilty of this vicious and horrible crime.

The next time I saw Judge Nix, I asked him why he'd said all that to the jury. Nix told me that when Cockfield had first been arrested, nine years before, he, Nix, was then a defense attorney. Cockfield's uncle had come to him to ask him to handle the case, but other members of the family had gone to Cecil Moore.

Nix never did handle any part of the case but he did

know about Willard Cockfield and the crime nine years before. That's all he told me, and you can draw your own conclusions concerning just what he knew about Willard Cockfield nine years before.

I met Cockfield again when I was at Holmesburg Prison to see a couple of clients. He told me he thought I had done a very fine job in court, and now that he knew I was handling the defense, he might want to retain me sometime.

Needless to say, I've seen Cecil Moore again, although the next time I was scheduled to try a case against him as a DA, Moore protested mightily in court. He said he did not want to have me representing the commonwealth because of "the kind of tactics" I "stooped to" in the course of a trial. Well, all I can say is I'm sure Cecil Moore recognized the kind of tactics I used and knew who I'd learned them from—and I'm grateful to him.

9

Good Publicity

I'll use anything I can to win a case. I'll use publicity whenever I ethically can.

A lot has been said and written about the way publicity can prejudice a fair trial—and it can. Some defense lawyers say that if the newspapers start writing about your client or even about the type of crime he's involved in, you've got an automatic dead duck, a squashed squab. No chance.

However, public opinion can go both ways. Sometimes public opinion can help a defendant, not hurt him. I think public opinion saved Danny Kellenbenz's skin.

Danny Kellenbenz, with his younger brother Philip, committed a particularly vicious murder. He shot a seventy-year-old neighborhood druggist, right in front of the man's wife, in an attempted holdup. The old woman was pushed around, and when she cried out in agony for someone to call a doctor, Danny ripped the telephone from the wall and then ran away.

You would think the public would howl to lynch this kid—the electric chair would be too good for him. But it didn't work out that way.

Danny Kellenbenz was just an average city kid. He grew up in a neighborhood where the families are large and the houses are small. His mom worked in a supermarket; his dad, in a factory. One of his brothers quit the seminary to go to medical school. Another brother was a Philadelphia cop. Nobody would have picked Danny Kellenbenz to become a dope addict and a murderer. But Danny became an addict in Vietnam and a murderer shortly after he got back.

Danny wasn't the only GI to take up drugs in 'Nam. You could get 95 percent pure heroin there as easily as walking into a barber shop. It was cheap. You could get high just by smoking the stuff, and that's what Danny did. That's what a lot of guys—bored or scared or angry or hurting from wounds—did. Danny came home with a chest full of medals, including the Purple Heart. He wanted to kick his drug habit when he got back but he didn't know how. He went to a Veterans Administration hospital for help, but it was 1969 and the government hadn't yet recognized the drug addiction that had developed in Vietnam. There were no clinics—methadone or otherwise—for the likes of Danny Kellenbenz. Danny sold everything he owned to raise money for junk.

But it wasn't enough. In the United States, it wasn't easy to come by the stuff. And it wasn't 95 percent here, it was 5 percent. It had to be injected. It had to be hustled for, and Danny Kellenbenz didn't know how to hustle.

Danny, then twenty-one years old, had been home about a year when his situation reached the crisis stage.

During that year, he had gotten married. The night before the holdup-murder, Danny called his mother.

"I've got some good news and some bad news," he said lightly. "The good news is that Peggy is pregnant. The bad news is that I feel sick."

Actually, all the news was disastrous for Danny. He had just finished his first day on a new job—making candles at a waxworks—and he couldn't hold that job if he felt sick. (An addict who can't get a fix suffers from stomach cramps, watering eyes, a runny nose, and dizziness.) Danny couldn't afford to support a family and a habit. He couldn't keep the family if he didn't hold a job.

Danny decided he had to get hold of some Dilaudid. He'd been told that this drug, available only by prescription, would dull his craving for heroin and enable him to shake the habit.

A lot of people believed that five years ago.

Dilaudid is a painkiller, chemically similar to morphine and just as addictive. Ironically, heroin was first introduced in this country as a cure for morphine addiction—and here was a morphinelike drug being touted as a cure for heroin addiction.

Dilaudid's only advantages over heroin, as it has turned out, are that it does not produce euphoria, requires a smaller dose, and is cheaper—if you can get it. Methadone is similar in that it, too, does not produce euphoria and requires only a small dose for effect. But it also is addictive.

Be that as it may, all Danny knew was that this drug was supposed to be able to help him and that he wanted it. He went to his brother Philip, seventeen, to ask if he knew a place to get it. Philip had held various after-school jobs in drugstores.

"I know a place," said Philip. "The people there are old and they won't give you any trouble." Philip, who was very close to his brother, volunteered to accompany him.

Next Danny went to visit a boyhood friend, twenty-year-old Sid Gorsky (not his real name). He wanted to borrow a starter pistol that the boys used to play with when both were small. Gorsky no longer had the starter pistol; now he had a regular .22-caliber revolver that shot live bullets. And he loaned both the revolver and the bullets to his pal.

Gorsky later admitted that he knew Danny was an addict, and that he at least imagined what Danny planned to do with the gun.

Yet, he just handed it over. Figure that one out. Gorsky could have been prosecuted as an accessory to murder, but he wasn't.

The two boys walked to Herbert Roth's drugstore. Roth was president of the Philadelphia Association of Pharmacists. He had once hired Phil Kellenbenz to run errands.

It was about eleven on a Saturday morning.

They walked through a deserted schoolyard. Danny put the bullets into Gorsky's gun and test-fired it. Philip got very nervous at that. "You won't shoot him, will you?" he asked Danny. "If he gives you any trouble, just grab him."

In his confession Danny described what happened next:

"Philip pointed the store out and I went in. Philip stayed outside and said he would wait for me. I went into the store, walked to the counter in the back. Philip told me that was where he kept the Dilaudid. I had the gun I'd borrowed in my pocket. When I got to the counter, the old man came from the back and asked if he could help me.

" 'Yes,' I said. 'I want Dilaudid.'

"He stooped to look and then he noticed the gun. He started stalling and I said, 'Hurry up, I'm sick. I need the pills. I don't want to hurt you. Just give me the pills and I'll leave.'

"But he stood up and grabbed for the gun.

"And then he grabbed for a telephone behind him . . . he was yelling into the phone that he wanted the police. I tried to wrestle the phone away and I still had the gun in my hand. He reached for the gun again. We struggled.

"He was hollering for his wife then . . . telling her to call the police. I don't think she understood what was happening. I dropped the phone and then the gun went off. He fell and didn't say anything. He just moaned.

"Philip came in and I told him to look for the drug. I told the woman to open the register and she did and I reached in and got some bills. I started to leave and realized I'd dropped my sunglasses, so I went back to get them. The woman was on the phone. I pulled the phone off the wall and then went out of the store."

Danny didn't know that Roth was dead, but he knew he'd shot him. He and Philip ran to a friend's house a few blocks away and asked if they could call a taxi. They waited until the taxi came; then Danny dropped his brother off and told the driver to take him to his apartment. En route he spotted another friend to whom he owed money. He asked the driver to stop, paid over six dollars, and then went home.

Odd behavior, to say the least. People do not seem to do what you expect them to do after a murder. Danny did finally get back to his apartment and told Peggy what had happened. She couldn't believe it.

They turned on both radio and television to get some news, and learned that Roth was dead. Then they just lay in bed feeling sick.

Two friends came by and told Danny his brother Philip had been picked up for questioning by the police. One of the boys offered to get rid of the gun—he'd take it and throw it away. Danny Kellenbenz certainly had loyal friends.

Another younger brother, Eddie, fifteen, came by to go to dinner with Danny and Peggy. They went to a diner. As they came out a police wagon stopped beside them and the officer asked their names. He took them to the police station, where Danny admitted what he'd done.

The case got the full treatment in the press. The city's pharmacists demanded the death penalty for Danny and better police protection for themselves. The DA promised to seek the full penalty of law. I concede that the first publicity was not anything in Danny Kellenbenz's favor.

The DA had evidence against Danny coming out of his ears. When Danny had first asked Philip for advice about a place to rob, Philip was at a friend's house. So now that friend would be able to testify that the crime was premeditated. Test-firing the gun in the schoolyard was further evidence—why test a gun you don't plan to use? The police rounded up all those loyal friends—loyal until they were told that unless they cooperated and testified properly they would be held as accessories. They cooperated.

The young man who had offered to hide the murder weapon now offered to find it. He led police to a hollow log in the park.

You wouldn't need more than that to win a conviction —and the DA had more than that, plenty more.

Elizabeth Roth, the sixty-nine-year-old widow, was

able to identify both boys. She knew Philip because he had worked in the store. She said she had pleaded with the boys to get help for her husband but all they'd cared about was robbing the cash register.

There were at least six witnesses to the getaway. There were five neighborhood teenagers on the street, all of whom knew Phil Kellenbenz. When they identified him, they weren't trying to remember the face of a stranger, they were recognizing someone they knew. It is very tough to refute an identification like that. And then, of course, there was the cabdriver who picked the boys up and dropped each one at his home.

Every detail was damning. And every damning detail was corroborated by several witnesses. The DA was going to show that my man was the most cold-blooded killer imaginable, a "drug-crazed punk" ripping the phone from the widow's hands, coolly stopping the taxi to repay a debt with stolen money. I could honestly say that this was not the most promising case I'd ever had.

When Danny and Philip were first arrested, the court appointed attorneys to represent them. The Kellenbenz family was upset about the attorney appointed for Danny because he was essentially a civil lawyer, and they rightly felt that if anybody needed an experienced criminal lawyer, Danny did.

I was hired as Danny's lawyer by the family on the strength of the recommendation of another client, Pebbles Finarelli, whom Danny met in prison while awaiting trial. (Pebbles had the highest regard for me, as well he should have, considering the mess *he* was in and what I did for him.) Anyway, the family obviously had little money, but I said if they could get four thousand dollars together, I'd take the case. They paid me fifty dollars a week and I knew it was coming right out of their food budget. But hell, if I hadn't taken it, *I* wouldn't have had a food budget.

The first thing I did was stall. Stalling is the defense attorney's first defense. If you don't know what to do, at least you keep the DA from doing what he wants to do. And while I was stalling, I was looking for some mitigating factor that would soften the jury's view of Danny. Philip wasn't in much danger of the chair (the death penalty was very much legal then). He was only helping his older brother. He hadn't pulled the trigger. Danny was in plenty of danger.

There was, of course, his background. He came from such a fine family. His mother told me how well all the kids got along. She told me Danny used to bring home gifts for her and for his sisters. That was nice but I couldn't really see a jury going all soft and mushy just because a murderer was kind to his mother.

And there was his experience in Vietnam. If Danny was indeed a drug-crazed punk, he'd obviously become that in Vietnam. Maybe a jury would take that into consideration . . . and maybe not.

I pondered legal means of slipping that Vietnam testimony into the trial. I had better explain that in Pennsylvania, unlike many other states, criminal responsibility is determined by the McNaughton rule; i.e., if you are sane enough to know right from wrong, you must bear responsibility for whatever you do. (In recent years the rule has been modified to permit psychiatric testimony that might show the crime was committed in the "heat of passion," but that wouldn't have applied to Danny anyway.)

You cannot claim you didn't know what you were doing

because you were under the influence of alcohol or drugs if you voluntarily imbibed the alcohol or took the drugs. On the other hand, if someone tied you up and forced a fifth down your throat or injected you with a drug that put you out of your mind—if you were involuntarily subjected to those influences and *then* committed a crime, you would be totally absolved.

I toyed with the idea of trying to claim that Danny was involuntarily drugged because of his service in Vietnam. He had volunteered for the Army at the age of seventeen, but he was involuntarily wounded. Therefore, his subsequent use of heroin should be considered involuntary intoxication because it was done under duress and beyond his control. I have heard of wilder bits of legal legerdemain. If it at least succeeded in getting Danny's Vietnam experience in front of the jury, I thought there was a good chance that at least there would be no death penalty.

The problem was that under ordinary circumstances his Vietnam experience would not be considered relevant to the case. I would ask the defendant, "Were you honorably discharged and wounded and received four medals in Vietnam?" And the DA would object and the judge would sustain him. "How is that relevant to whether or not he committed this robbery-murder in January of 1970?" I was trying to think up a legal theory that would make it relevant.

Meanwhile I'm stalling. I'm asking for medical tests; I'm writing away for military records; I'm hoping like hell that something turns up something. And I'm becoming more and more convinced that the Vietnam thing is relevant, and what's more, it is the only defense I've got.

With the help of the Kellenbenz family, I got in touch with Danny's old service buddies.

I started getting letters from them that told a story about a brave kid who never shirked his share of danger, who used to volunteer for night patrols, who'd get wounded, get patched up, and get right back to his unit.

Carmine Malito, who was Danny's sergeant in Vietnam, even visited me in my office. He showed up with his wife and he was beautiful. He told me Danny had volunteered for more night patrols than anyone else in the platoon. Danny never said no, sir. He wished he could've had more young men like Danny Kellenbenz.

Malito also told me that Danny had been wounded in the head.

Things were beginning to look brighter.

When I visited Danny in prison to talk about his case, one of the first things he told me was that he had blacked out during the shooting. I showed him his confession, in which he had clearly related every detail. He told me that some of those details had been helpfully supplied by the police. He maintained that actually he'd blacked out.

Now, *everybody* says he blacked out at the critical moment. It's a stock answer. It's transparent. But when you don't have anything else, you take a little time to investigate.

I got hold of his prison record, and lo, he was having blackouts while in prison. (Of course, you would have to wonder if he was deliberately having blackouts to impress his attorney—but he did report them.)

He also made some serious suicide attempts in prison —serious enough that I didn't think they were just attempts to impress anybody.

I asked for an electroencephalogram—a test of the brain waves. The results were inconclusive but some of the tests showed disturbance. Maybe the head wound had affected Danny's behavior; maybe the wound had led to his addiction. I couldn't prove it, but maybe a jury would at least think about it. And Carmine Malito's testimony would certainly help.

I wrote to the Pentagon to get Danny's medical records. They sent back his discharge papers and some other records but not the medical records. I called the center for military personnel files in St. Louis and they said the records had been sent. If we ever have to win a war on the Army's record-keeping system, we're in real trouble. I wrote to Pennsylvania Senator Richard Schweiker and asked him to help get the records, and he tried. The Army sent some court-martial records. Oh, that was a big help. Now I find out my guy has had some problems in the Army, sold stuff on the black market.

Oh, well, I still had Malito.

But even better, I had a changing public climate on the problem of drug addiction. Months had gone by. In 1969 nobody talked about the drug problem created in Vietnam. By 1971 it seemed no one talked of anything else.

I began clipping news articles from the papers and before long I had a drawer full. A Republican congressman from Connecticut who had gone to Vietnam for the House Foreign Affairs Committee said, "A soldier going to South Vietnam today runs a greater risk of becoming a heroin addict than a battle casualty."

Two Senate committees opened hearings and veterans flocked to Washington to testify how they'd taken drugs out of pain or fear or boredom and that when they'd returned to the States hooked, there had been no help for them.

The American Medical Association began demanding federal programs to help addicts. The Army began a half-hearted "amnesty" program in which an addict who turned himself in would receive treatment instead of a dishonorable discharge. And the Veterans Administration began to set up clinics for addicts—the kind that Danny Kellenbenz had sought and didn't find.

Meanwhile, I was running back and forth to court all the time because the district attorney's office was trying to push the case to trial. The DA was getting static from the pharmacists and from the widow: Why isn't this case being tried? The case wasn't tried because Moldovsky kept asking for postponements in order to have tests, get records, locate buddies (and to hope the public was getting more upset about the Vietnam drug problem).

And one day, as I was running to court, I bumped into Jon Steinberg. O Happy Day! Jon Steinberg was an administrative aide to the district attorney and an old friend of my brother's. We caught up on old times and I told him I had a case involving a drug addict and he told me he was very interested in drug-addiction problems. In fact, when Steinberg was in the Army—which wasn't that long ago, since he's only thirty now—he did a study on marijuana use by GIs for the 44th Medical Brigade. At first the military tried to squelch the study but Jon later won a Bronze Star for doing it. Anyway, Jon was sympathetic to addicts who, he felt, were forced to crime because of their habit. He felt the easy availability of heroin in Vietnam might well have been a Communist ploy to defeat the Americans. How about that?

Anyway, Jon told me about a TV show a friend of his

from ABC was working on—a documentary on the whole Vietnam drug-addiction scene. So naturally I suggested that my client Daniel Kellenbenz would make an excellent subject for the documentary.

The next thing you know, it had all been arranged with the warden of Holmesburg Prison that a crew from ABC would arrive to interview Danny there. Normally outsiders can't get into Holmesburg, but, after all, here was the district attorney's administrative aide involved, so it must be okay, right? Frank Reynolds narrated the show but Ron Miller, who covered the Vietnam War for ABC, came to Philadelphia to do the interview.

I was on the show, too, and everything was going fine. And then Danny started to relate how he had killed his lieutenant.

I practically dropped my teeth—I was that shocked. I've got it all planned that Danny is going to get sympathy because of his drug habit, which drove him to this terrible crime, and here he is confessing to another killing right in front of the whole country.

Danny got going and didn't stop!

"I was out on patrol and I hadn't had a chance to shoot up all day. I was sick and nervous. My hands were shaking. Suddenly we were under attack. It was dark. For a second the sky lit up and I saw a man in front of me. I thought he was coming at me. I opened fire. The man fell on me . . . the blood was gushing all over me. The sky lit up again when a mortar fired and I saw it was an American lieutenant, I'd killed my own lieutenant."

I asked Danny to recall how he'd taken up drugs in Vietnam, how he'd gotten hooked on scag. Danny said he wasn't sure. His officers used to pass out the stuff to keep the troops calm when they were afraid. And sometimes he took it to dull the pain in his head.

The more I heard the more convinced I was that Vietnam really had screwed this kid up, that Vietnam was responsible for both Roth's death and that of the unnamed lieutenant.

And I made a pitch just that way to First Assistant District Attorney Richard Sprague. I wanted Sprague to drop the murder-one charge and lower it to something that would demand a jail term—not a death penalty.

"This guy was sick; he's a goddamn hero. His own officers hooked him and he's out of his head with shrapnel wounds. He's the kind of person who'd bare his own soul to help save others. And if you don't accept a lesser charge, you may take a chance that I'll get the kid off free."

I must have been arguing pretty good because Sprague agreed to lower the charge. And Sprague practically never agrees to do that. When it comes to murder, Sprague is a ball of righteous indignation. Make that two balls.

I don't think Sprague believed for a minute that I'd ever win an acquittal, and I didn't believe that either. I think he did realize that I could give him a hell of a fight now . . . you couldn't just call Danny Kellenbenz a drug-crazed punk and automatically win murder one. Maybe he just decided what did the DA's office need with the aggravation of Moldovsky and his cockamamie theories and his medical testimony? And after all, the defendant's brother is a cop, and the defendant—that son-of-a-bitch —is a TV hero.

And, oh yes, there was one other little thing.

While Danny Kellenbenz was in Holmesburg, there was a prison riot.

The usual causes—racial tension, lousy conditions. The district attorney's office was very interested in having the leader of the riot convicted. I discussed this with Danny: maybe he knew something about it, maybe he could help the DA and then maybe the DA would help him.

It turned out that the leader of the riot, a guy named Brown, had made some remarks which Danny had overheard but didn't take seriously at the time. Danny agreed to testify against Brown, and when Brown learned about that, he pleaded guilty.

So Danny had that going for him, too. He not only went on TV to help solve the dope problem, he was willing to testify for the commonwealth to help root out antisocial behavior in prison.

Of course, Danny wasn't the only prisoner willing to help the DA if the DA would help him. And I was forced to write a letter to Danny warning him to be cautious while talking to his fellow prisoners.

"Your trial prosecutor," I wrote him, "has gathered evidence that you have been involved in LSD smuggling at Holmesburg and that you have bragged how you and your lawyer will come up with something by making believe you are crazy and blaming what happened on the war and that in not too many years you will walk out. Now, none of this may be true, but certain other prisoners will be ready to swear to this in return for promises of leniency for them."

In short, both sides fenced around for a while, but in the end the Kellenbenz case never went to a jury.

The DA's office agreed to a plea of second degree and both boys pleaded guilty. Danny was sentenced to ten to forty years and Philip to ten to twenty-five. Under our furlough and prerelease statutes, a well-behaved prisoner can be prereleased when half his minimum term is served. Under prerelease you live at home and report once a week to a treatment center. Both boys continued their educations in jail and are considered good candidates for early release after five years.

Would I have compromised on murder one if I'd been handling the prosecution? Never! In my opinion, the DA had more than enough evidence to win conviction of both brothers, no matter how hard a defense attorney tried to stir up sympathy for them. If I'd been DA I would have stressed the fact that *after* the shooting, the boys did not try to get help for the old man . . . that Danny had pulled the phone out of the wall. I'm pretty sure I could have gotten them the chair.

Would that have been better justice than what I arranged as a defense attorney? I don't know.

10

The Jailhouse Client

One of the problems a criminal lawyer has to face that other kinds of lawyers do not is that all of his clients cannot make appointments and come to see him in his own comfortable office. Some clients he has to see in surroundings that are not comfortable at all. They are in jail. They are there either because they were not granted bail or, more likely, because they couldn't make the bail that was granted.

I am never happy when my client is in jail. It is not just the damn inconvenience of having to travel for an hour to get to him, although that's part of it. I also have to make arrangements in advance, sign in with prison guards, get a quick frisk at the gate, and wait in a bare cubicle until the guards find my client and bring him to me.

At Holmesburg Prison, which has all the appeal of a medieval dungeon, the attorney's interview area is next to the visitor's area. So you sit, going over the facts with your client, while other prisoners and their families or friends are screaming back and forth through little mesh screens.

If your client has a hearing scheduled, he will be brought down in a sheriff's van from the prison early in the morning and locked up in a cellroom in City Hall until required to make an appearance. And once his appearance is made, he goes back to the cellroom to wait until all the prisoners who have been brought down that day are assembled so they can be taken back to prison together.

So if you want to see this guy, say at the lunch break or after the trial has recessed for the day, you can't just huddle with him in the hallway outside the courtroom or run over to your office with him or grab a quick cup of coffee, you have to go to the cellroom and apply to see him.

And he'll be brought out with his hands handcuffed in front of him. The fact that the handcuffs are in front is considered a great reform of recent years. Until not too long ago, the prisoner would have had his hands handcuffed behind him. You can imagine how difficult it was for somebody to spend an hour or so going over important evidence and procedures with you while sitting on a hard chair, hands cuffed behind him.

This is one of the great advantages of being well-to-do enough to be out on bail: you don't have to take this kind of treatment.

Bad enough you have to see your client in the cellroom, but sometimes you really have to outflank the DA to even do that. If it's a serious case, the DA may try to have the sheriffs whisk the defendant back into the van and back to the prison before the attorney can make it upstairs to ask to see him.

The prisoners are taken up to the cellroom in a special

back elevator and taken down to the sheriff's vans through a fire-tower emergency elevator.

But the defense attorney has to use the regular elevators, which stop at every floor and which don't come just because you ring. The attorney has to sign in, get past security, etc., etc. And he may then be told, "Oh, Herman Klutz. Sorry, he was just taken out."

Sometimes I have had to get a judge to sign an order directing that my particular client not be removed from the cellroom until the last van goes out—about six or seven in the evening—and that he be available to see me. And then I call the captain of the cellroom and tell him I have this order.

It's a great pain for the lawyer but obviously it's no great advantage for the client either. If he's got a lawyer who doesn't go to a lot of trouble to see him, he doesn't see his lawyer much.

The difficulty of lawyer and client getting together can be the least of the problems faced by the client who is in custody. He can't, for instance, help his own case by doing his own investigation.

I had a client named Jerry Smith who was accused of some minor theft—the crime isn't that important—but he claimed to have an alibi. He was with a guy he'd met in a bar. They'd gone a few places that night.

So naturally I want him to find this guy, to find out if anybody else saw him that night who will remember him. Now maybe if you have money you hire private investigators to do all of this for you. But if you don't have money, you can probably do it yourself—if you are on the outside, that is. You find somebody who says, "Yeah, Peter. . . . No, I don't know where he lives . . . but I think he has an aunt on Somerset Street near Twenty-seventh."

The one thing that Jerry Smith had to help him find this guy that neither a private investigator nor I had was the memory of what this guy looked like. The minute he spotted him, he recognized him.

And, in the eyes of a jury, there is a kind of taint on a prisoner. He must be a dangerous man, or why is he not out on bail?

Theoretically, the jury is not supposed to know that your client is a prisoner. In fact, it is grounds for mistrial if anybody even mentions it. That's a far cry from the days when a defendant came to his trial in his prison uniform. The rule today is that every defendant must be in "civilian" clothes.

A conscientious judge will make sure that the defendant is present in the courtroom and seated next to his attorney before he permits the jury to be seated. But some judges don't even think about that. And what happens is that the jury is present, the DA is present, and the defense attorney is present, but the accused is not.

And then, about ten minutes later, the door to a little room adjoining the courtroom opens and out comes the defendant, and about ten feet behind him walks a sheriff. And every juror knows, even if nobody is allowed to say, that the guy has been hauled in from the jug.

When a man is free on bail, he hangs around the corridors with his family. The jury can see him there. He looks like a regular guy, not a dangerous person at all. And it makes an impression.

It's bad enough to try to defend someone who is in jail because he is accused of a crime. It's worse to defend somebody who is accused of committing a crime while in prison. Not only is a jury going to be suspicious about your client—if he's so nice, how come he's in jail—but also about your client's witnesses. Suppose his "alibi" is the word of his cellmate—but his cellmate has been convicted of a crime even worse than his. He is in big trouble.

That's the kind of problem I had with Carl Jamieson.

Jamieson was in the Philadelphia House of Correction doing six to twenty-three months on possession of heroin —not pushing, possessing. He was twenty-four, had a wife and baby girl, and seemed to be a pretty straight fellow, overall. But Carl was accused with five other inmates by a junkie named Ernie Roundtree of gang-raping him in a cell.

Now, this whole matter of sexual assaults in prison is a sordid business that prison officials would just as soon not discuss. Everybody knows that when men have no access to women, they sometimes decide that access to men will have to do. And if you get an aggressive homosexual in custody, he can really make the jailhouse rock.

It isn't unknown for a gay guy to get himself arrested for disorderly conduct or some other minor offense so he can catch five or ten days in jail and come out smiling.

However, if somebody is sexually assaulted who doesn't want to be, he can make a big stink about it. He can argue cruel and unusual punishment. After all, he's a prisoner, he's in the commonwealth's custody, and the commonwealth is responsible for him. And besides, it isn't good publicity for the city if he files a suit or something and the public finds out about all the assaults that go on.

Anyway, this Ernie Roundtree was twenty years old, a big guy, and he claimed that six fellow prisoners, including his cellmates, had raped him anally and forced him to have oral sex. The six claimed that was just wishful thinking on Ernie's part because he was gay anyway.

They said he'd had relations with a lot of prisoners without complaining—including his cellmates.

Roundtree had complained a few years before of a sexual attack while in prison, and both the defendants in that case pleaded guilty for probation.

That didn't prove anything to me because I know that when you're in prison you figure you might as well cop a plea if there's an agreement not to add to your sentence, rather than try to plead innocence and take a chance that you'll be found guilty and sentenced to a longer stretch.

When a con's only defense is his own word, he doesn't necessarily expect to be believed.

Roundtree's cellmates denied the attack completely. They said Roundtree had put in a request to be moved out of that cell because his cellmates had been riding him for sloppiness, but the request had been refused. Then he made a request to be transferred out of the House of Correction entirely, and that was refused.

The cellmates said Roundtree was only causing problems to get himself out of there. And that's been known to happen too. A guy claims he's afraid to stay in that prison because the friends of the men he's accused are out to get him. So the prison authorities have to "protect him" by transferring him.

Prisoners also use accusations against each other as a means of "getting even" for something, or as a way of causing so many problems for the prison authorities that they'll be happy to recommend early parole just to get rid of the troublemaker.

Well, it's one thing to know that these things frequently happen and another to prove what happened in a particular case. My client—courtesy of a court appointment

—was not one of the cellmates, but he also denied having anything to do with Ernie Roundtree.

I started checking and I found that Roundtree never even reported this alleged offense until four days after it was supposed to have happened. And when he filed, he claimed to have been assaulted four other times that he hadn't bothered to report.

That sounded pretty phony to me. But the cellmates went to trial and the jury convicted them. The trial had been held in front of Judge Eddie Rosenwald, who 's a deliverer of heavy sentences. That fact apparently convinced another codefendant to change his plea to guilty in return for a short sentence of four to twenty-three months.

Before Carl Jamieson went on trial, I decided to go to the prison to view the area where the assault was supposed to have happened. Roundtree claimed he shouted for help. So I wanted to know where the guard would have been stationed when this happened. I wanted to know if the guard could have heard the shouts and I also wanted to ask the guard if my client could have been out of his cell and in Roundtree's cell at the time the assault was alleged to have happened.

But when I got to the prison, they wouldn't let me into the cellblock. Another disadvantage of the prisoner-client!

The prison authorities don't consider the prison public territory, and if they don't want to cooperate with a prisoner's lawyer, they won't.

Actually, that turned out to be a break, because I demanded to see the lieutenant, then the captain, then the deputy, and finally the warden—all of whom refused to let me go to the cellblock. I don't know what they thought I'd see up there.

I got a judge on the phone and the judge talked to the warden, but it didn't do any good. The warden said he'd only accept a judicial order if it was in writing. So I made a huge stink about all that to the DA's office. I was going to subpoena the warden and every damn guard in the place; I'd get a jury into the prison. What are they hiding? Why can't my client have a proper defense? Etc., etc.

So finally the DA's office just agreed to drop prosecution against Carl Jamieson. It was easier to do that than have the whole House of Correction under investigation. And, of course, it was easier for me too.

No matter how you look at it, being in prison is a big disadvantage.

And that is why bail is such a continuing controversy. Constitutionally and legally, bail is required only to ensure the appearance of the accused at his trial.

It is not supposed to be a means of punishment, although it is not unknown for the lower-court judge to set a high bail that will ensure that the accused stays in jail for a while even if there's good reason to believe he'll later be acquitted.

Generally, the amount of bail is determined pretty much by the offense charged. For instance, a larceny, with no prior record involved, would have bail at three hundred to a thousand dollars. A rape or a strong-arm robbery would bring a bail of three thousand to ten thousand dollars. But a magistrate or municipal-court judge has a lot of latitude, and if he wants to put on a high bail he can do it. The client can appeal the bail, of course, but meanwhile he either raises the higher bail or stays inside.

And bail costs money. If you go to a bail bondsman,

you pay 10 percent of whatever the bail is for him to guarantee it, and you never get that 10 percent back. In effect, if you have to get bail, you pay a "fine" even if you are acquitted.

A few years ago, the city of Philadelphia went into the bail-bonding business itself to stop some of the worst abuses of the bondsmen—abuses I assume still go on in other places in the state and in other states. There was a lot of fee-splitting with attorneys; in fact, you couldn't get many cases as a criminal lawyer in the old days unless you had some kind of agreement with a bondsman.

Some attorneys had direct investments in bonding companies, others had kickback arrangements, but the fact was that criminal-law business in the city was pretty much tied up by just a few. The bondsmen had runners, or agents, in all the police stations. And when somebody got arrested, the runners would immediately contact the family to arrange for bail. There was a lot of competition because bail is a multimillion-dollar business.

Then, of course, the guy would need a lawyer and he wouldn't necessarily know any, so the "nice" bail bondsman would fix him up with a mouthpiece.

When I first became a defense lawyer, a friend of mine said one of his best friends was a bail bondsman, and just out of friendship this bondsman was going to see that I got business. He gave me the business all right. The first day I went over to the roundhouse (police headquarters), one of this bondsman's runners came up to me with a client.

"This gentleman here got popped with a couple of bags of heroin and I told him you'd get the charge washed out for three hundred fifty dollars. Here's the money."

Then he excused himself from the "gentleman" and took me aside.

"Here's your hundred seventy-five and here's my hundred seventy-five."

"Wait a minute," I said. "You can have the whole three hundred fifty and find yourself another guy."

That is not my idea of the practice of law. Aside from the illegality of the whole thing, here is this agent telling me I'm going to get a "not guilty" and I don't even know the facts of the case. He looks like the big cheese and I look like the stooge. On top of that, I'm the one who would have to pay income taxes on three hundred and fifty dollars (since the client would think he paid it all to me), and the runner would get a clear hundred and seventy-five.

Yet there were lawyers who made a whole career out of this kind of thing. They got enough cases to make it lucrative.

You might ask how the runner knew the case would be washed out, how he could promise that to the client. Well, could be the bondsman had the political power to influence a judge, and also enough power to get the case to the judge of his choice. Or could be the agent was experienced enough to recognize a "bad arrest" when he saw one and knew that a lawyer pointing out a couple of technical deficiencies would be all that was required.

I don't know.

I did find a good, honest bondsman with whom I could work on a professional basis. I send him clients and he sends me clients and that's it.

But, mostly, I think I was able to break into the business because the city now provides most of the bail on a routine basis—no favorites.

The city gives a very good deal on bail and it particularly benefits the poor. Like the independent bondsmen, the city also charges 10 percent to go bail, but unlike the bondsmen, once the case is tried, the city gives 90 percent of that 10 percent back. If the bail is, say, ten thousand dollars, both the bondsmen and the city charge a thousand dollars. (The city adds a three-dollar processing fee.) But after the trial, the accused having shown up as required, the city gives nine hundred dollars back while the bondsmen give back nothing.

This has driven some bondsmen out of business, but not all. The private bondsmen have survived by lowering their rates a little, and also because they are willing to take as bail security some things the city won't take. The city accepts a lien on a house up to the assessed value (and if you owe a mortgage on part of that value, that part doesn't count) or cold cash. A bondsman may work it out to take stock, or jewelry—or your girlfriend.

It may sound like a real ripoff for the bondsmen to charge 10 percent if the city can charge what eventually amounts to 1 percent, but it isn't that bad.

After all, the bondsman has expenses. He has to pay his agents. He has to pay bounty hunters to find guys who have skipped bail on him. The bondsman doesn't lose any money if he can produce the jumper within thirty days of the missed court appearance. So the bondsman looks pretty hard for these people, and bondsmen in different cities help each other. If a bail jumper is located in another state, a bounty hunter just picks him up and puts him in a car and brings him back. No extradition is required, because to get bail, you sign a contract saying that if you skip, you can be brought back from anywhere. But all this is expensive. The city, of course, has police already on the payroll to do this.

The city went into the bail business not just to lower the fees for bail to help out the poor but also to make sure that more people got bail. The bail bondsmen sometimes took a personal dislike to a would-be customer for some reason and wouldn't go bail for him. Worse than that, the bondsmen had a little fraternity, so that to be blacklisted by one was to be blacklisted by all. The bondsmen had all kinds of reasons for refusing bail—some logical, but some not.

The major reason bail would be refused was simply that the bondsman considered the defendant a poor risk. Somebody who is poor, who owns no property, who is also jobless, perhaps, would be considered risky since such a person has no ties that would force him to stay around. A bondsman might blacklist someone who failed to show for a hearing even if there was a legitimate reason for failing to show—such as being in an accident or in the hospital or in jail.

So the hapless soul who couldn't get bail would have to await trial in prison, sometimes for months, sometimes for years. And that's the vicious circle: the guy who isn't free has a poorer chance of getting permanently free than the guy who is temporarily free on bail.

11

The Gun Game

You don't have to deal with crime very long before you realize that the mere presence of a gun is sometimes the only difference between murder and simple assault and battery. I can't remember a single case I've ever had in which the victim was strangled or punched to death. Not that these things don't happen, but they are rare. I can, however, think of a whole stream of cases in which, if not for the easy availability of a gun, the worst that would have happened to the victim would have been a punch in the mouth or a kick in the balls.

I don't want to give the impression that I'm against guns, because I'm not. I recognize gun ownership as an intrinsic part of American life, more American even than apple pie. A lot of people can't sleep if they don't have a weapon under their pillow. A lot of people don't feel whole if they don't own a gun. And in a poor, tough neighborhood in the city, it is axiomatic that he who does not pack a rod risks packing it in, period. Two guys get into a fight in a bar, for instance; one reaches meaning-fully to his belt. In some locales, if the other can't reach just as meaningfully toward his belt, he can't even hope for a standoff.

No, I am not against guns; I have one myself. But I think Americans have to accept the idea that since guns are a part of the culture, you have to expect them to go off now and then. I have gotten some of my nicest clients that way—people who ordinarily would not get into significant trouble, people who are just ordinary citizens, except that they shot somebody.

I put both Robby Jenner and Herbert Glover in that category—both killed people they liked. Robby Jenner shot his best friend. Herbert Glover shot his mistress. As the saying goes: "With friends like that. . . ."

Robby Jenner, at the time he became my client, was twenty-two, a new father, an employee of a lumberyard, and the owner of a gun. He kept it in his house for pro-tection.

It seems that one night, Robby and his wife, Julia, were just finishing their dinner when one of Robby's buddies, Mickey Sanders, dropped by with a friend, Hardy Lyn-wood. Sanders and Lynwood took seats at the table and Mickey began kibitzing.

"Hey, Julia," he said. "Got any chicken for me?"

"Don't give that bum any chicken," said Robby. "That chicken is for me."

Julia good-naturedly put a plate in front of Sanders. Robby grabbed it. Mickey grabbed it back.

Robby and Mickey kept up a steady stream of insults and gibes and horseplay.

They were in the living room when the conversation got around to what would happen if an intruder tried to force his way into the apartment. Robby said he'd go for his gun, which he kept under the mattress of his bed.

"Man," said Sanders, "a burglar would be here and gone before you ever reached that gun. That's a stupid place to keep it. You could get a knife from the kitchen sooner than you could get that gun."

"The hell I could."

"You want to put your money where your mouth is?"

If those weren't the exact words, they're close. Anyway, the two decided to resolve that dispute with a little demonstration. At the count of three, Sanders would run to the kitchen and get a knife and Robby Jenner would run to the bedroom for his gun.

Sanders was quicker.

He got the knife and was back at the bedroom door just as Mickey was pulling the pistol from the bed. Julia and the baby were sitting on the bed watching television.

Mickey Sanders was triumphant.

Laughing, with the knife held above his head as if he were attacking, he came bounding into the bedroom. "I could cut you up and you'd still be looking to find the trigger."

Robby turned . . . gun in hand . . . and fired.

The bullet hit Mickey Sanders in the stomach.

Robby was stunned.

"Mickey! Oh my God!"

Robby and Hardy Lynwood took Sanders to the hospital immediately. At first they were not aware how seriously he'd been hurt. Sanders was still conscious, and the three decided they should tell hospital officials that they'd been walking down the street and a shot had come from a passing car. They told emergency-ward personnel they just hadn't been able to get the license plate.

However, later, when the police came to see Mickey, he related the actual story and told them that Robby had not meant to hurt him, that it had all been a joke.

If Mickey Sanders had lived, the worst that would have happened to Robby would have been a hearing for assault and battery. Mickey would show up at the hearing, say he didn't want to press charges, and that would be that.

But Mickey died the next day. And the police filed charges of murder.

Robby had, after all, never contended that he thought Mickey was seriously attacking him. It was never a question of self-defense. He couldn't claim the gun had gone off by accident; it hadn't fallen off the bed and discharged itself.

Robby claimed it was all a matter of horseplay gone awry, which was bad enough. The police, however, thought it was something worse.

The fact that Mickey had at first participated in the coverup story and the fact that he had absolved Robby on his deathbed were disregarded. After all, maybe Mickey was affected by the pain; maybe he didn't realize he was dying and was afraid of Robby. Funny thing about deathbed statements: you can never tell how the DA will introduce them in evidence. Sometimes they are declared to be merely the confused product of pain and drugs; and sometimes they are held up as the absolute of a man going to his maker. It sort of depends on what was said. In any case, if the DA interprets the statement one way, you can be sure the defense will explain it the other.

Two things made Robby look, at least in the eyes of the police, more like a deliberate murderer than a careless friend. One was his own admission, when he gave a statement, that he'd cocked the gun as he pointed it. Sure, he might well have cocked it automatically, in the excitement of the moment. But still, it meant he would've had to take *two steps* to shoot Mickey—cocking the gun and pulling the trigger. The second was the statement given by Hardy Lynwood, who told police that the two friends had been quarreling—that this quarrel had started over the chicken at dinner. A shooting after a quarrel, then, could mean anger or recklessness.

Robby insisted that he and Mickey were never quarreling. Sure they joshed each other all the time. Sure they challenged each other and shoved each other. But that's how they were.

Hardy Lynwood, who really didn't know Robby, wouldn't know that. Robby and Mickey had grown up together. They used to play fast-draw with toy guns together. Mickey had been best man at Robby's wedding. Mickey would know they weren't quarreling over chicken. Mickey would know it was all in fun. But Mickey was dead.

At the preliminary hearing, the judge decided to hold Robby Jenner on a charge of voluntary manslaughter: conviction could bring a maximum jail term of six to twelve years. Voluntary manslaughter indicates an act which, although not done with maliciousness, has as its natural and foreseeable consequence the taking of life. Like driving while drunk ... maybe you aren't malicious, but you are expected to foresee that a drunk driver might conceivably hit another car or a pedestrian; and if you do, you're responsible. In Robby's case, the charge was that he should have foreseen that cocking a gun, aiming it, and pulling the trigger could kill somebody.

The DA was willing to make a deal. If Robby would plead guilty to voluntary manslaughter, he'd be willing not to make any recommendation on sentence to the judge. That may not sound like much of an offer but sometimes that's very significant. You see, if the DA recommends a sentence of ten years and the judge decides on two years, the newspapers are going to point out the difference and some people will say that the judge is a softie, the judge is letting hardened criminals go free. Judges don't like that.

But if the DA just publicly "leaves it up to the judge," the implication for the public is that the prosecution has confidence this judge will do the "right thing."

However, in Jenner's case, I wanted to do better, so I insisted we go to trial, and I did my usual footwork in getting the case before the right judge. I refused to waive a jury until the case was scheduled before Judge Juanita Kidd Stout. Now, Judge Stout is known to whack out a tough sentence now and again, but she is also known to be considerate to family men, particularly those with no record.

I paid a visit to Lynwood . . . was he really so sure they had quarreled? Couldn't it have been, as Robby claimed, just fun and games? He conceded it could have been. And the DA never called Hardy Lynwood as a witness. Maybe he'd heard of my little visit; maybe he was aware Lynwood might change his story on the stand. I don't know. But the weight of the prosecution's case was really Robby's own statement about cocking the gun.

The weight of the defense case was really Robby himself. He didn't attempt to deny anything. He was so obviously withdrawn, morose, and upset by what he'd done—it came through.

The judge found him guilty of involuntary manslaughter, a misdemeanor that indicates only criminal negligence. It carries a maximum of three years in prison. The DA wanted at least a one-to-three-year term,

The judge deferred sentence until the probation department produced a report on Robby, and it was a gem. It talked of his happy marriage; it said he was a good husband and father, that his employer thought highly of him. Probation was recommended.

I pointed out to the judge that Mickey died requesting to see his friend Robby. That Robby had rushed to the hospital right after making bail on the initial assault charge, but Mickey was dead. I pointed out that Robby had gone to see Mickey's mother to tell her how sorry he was. "I am sure," I said, "that the mother of Michael Sanders would not want this boy sent to prison."

I think I got a little carried away saying that because I didn't know how Michael Sanders' mother felt. The judge decided to ask her—she was in the courtroom. I held my breath.

"I don't know where the fault lies," she said. "Robby will have to answer to God, and the judge."

The sentence was three years' probation. A good result, I think, for a man who really had lost his best friend. (It was a good result for me, too, because if Robby Jenner had gone to jail and lost his job, I don't know how he would have paid my fee.)

I wasn't able to avoid a jail sentence for Herbert Glover; but his case—although equally due to the presence of a gun, I think—was somewhat stickier than Robby Jenner's.

Herb Glover had a gun because of his job. He was a

deputy sheriff. He was also a former prison guard. It is one of the ironies of Herb Glover's life that he became a prisoner in the same prison in which he'd been a guard.

For years, Herb Glover considered himself a happily married man. He'd courted his wife for two years before they married. They got along fairly well; they had two kids, and the only thing that ever seemed to mar their relationship was money. They would quarrel over it.

After some of these quarrels, Glover wasn't so sure he was happily married. And it was after one of these quarrels that Glover met Joy Robinson. He had gone out by himself to a supper club where Joy was a waitress. He bantered with her, one thing led to another, and he asked her out. Joy was game. She was divorced from one husband, separated from another, had four children, and wasn't averse to having somebody pay a little attention to her.

It wasn't long before "happily married" Herb Glover was leading a double life—a wife in one house, a mistress in another. Not that Herb Glover paid Joy's rent, but he did buy her a trinket or two. In fact, if he thought his money troubles were tough before he met Joy, he knew what tough really was afterward. He even took a part-time job as a cabdriver to make his various ends meet.

Herb did not tell his wife about Joy and he didn't mention to Joy that he had a wife.

And that went on for three years! Then one Sunday when Herbert Glover was out walking with his family, who should walk by but Herb's other life. Oops.

Joy seemed to take it okay at first. She kidded a bit. But then she began putting the pressure on. Why didn't he get a divorce? He said he'd thought about it. What was he waiting for? Uh....

Unfortunately for all concerned, just about the time that Joy decided she wanted Herbert Glover to marry her, Herb Glover decided he wanted to end the affair and go back, full time, to his wife. Helen Glover had become pregnant with their third child. He began to feel guilty—his wife needed him, and he loved her. He made up his mind to straighten out and do right.

Easier said than done. He stayed away from Joy but Joy didn't like it. She'd call him at the sheriff's office and threaten to tell his wife. He'd placate her and promise to come over to see her.

Then one day in December 1970—Helen Glover was then eight and a half months' pregnant—Herb took a day off from work and went to see Joy. They had another roaring battle.

"Get out," she screamed. "Get out. Leave. But I'm going to fix you. I'm going to make sure your wife knows."

Joy went for the telephone. Her daughter Terry was at that time talking on it to her boyfriend.

"Get off the phone for a minute, Terry," her mother said. "I have to make an important call."

Joy Robinson went for the telephone.

Herb Glover went for his gun—the gun he carried because he was a deputy sheriff, and deputy sheriffs are always armed.

Herb later told me he just lost his head, blacked out, didn't realize what he was doing. He just wanted to stop Joy from calling his pregnant wife. So he shot her. Now maybe if he hadn't had a gun, he would just have grabbed her, shoved her, knocked her down. But he had a gun, and he whipped it out. . . .

He fired eleven times! His revolver only held six bullets, which meant that he'd had to reload. He said he didn't remember reloading. But he shot eleven times. Terry, who was seventeen years old, screamed and ran to her mother.

"What are you doing, Herb?" she said as she ran between them . . . and caught a bullet in her stomach. Luckily, she survived.

Terry's boyfriend, Richard Thomason, told police he hadn't hung up yet when Terry had handed the telephone to her mother and so he heard everything: the screams and the shots. Then he hung up and called the police.

Herb Glover went to see his wife and told her he had done something he had no business doing; then he called his captain at the sheriff's office and gave himself up.

Another bit of irony.

Herb Glover committed murder because he didn't want his wife to find out he'd had a mistress, so of course his wife not only found out about the mistress but also discovered that her husband was a murderer. How did she react? She did not rally to his side, that's for sure. She picked up the kids and she moved to Chicago. She didn't bother to visit him in jail. Herb Glover had made his bed and he was going to sleep in it—alone.

Herb had been in jail for a while when I took on his case. He'd had another attorney who wasn't moving for him. Not that Herb thought he was going to just get off, but he didn't like the uncertainty of not knowing what the sentence was going to be. He wanted to have the trial and get it over with. Herb knew me from when I'd been an assistant DA, and one day when I was at Holmesburg Prison visiting some other clients, he asked me how I'd feel about taking over his case. He didn't have any

money, it would have to be a court appointment. I said
I was for it if the court was.

Usually a destitute defendant does not get the lawyer
of his choice. The court will appoint a free lawyer, but
the client then has to take whomever he gets. Recently
one prisoner went into court to demand that F. Lee
Bailey be appointed to represent him. He'd heard of
Bailey and thought Bailey was equal to his case. The
judge did not take that too seriously.

However, Herb Glover got his wish—maybe because it
wasn't all that difficult to fulfill, and also because it was
a first-degree case.

Thereafter, on my trips to Holmesburg, I'd visit Herb
Glover, too. Holmesburg was where Glover had been a
guard and he knew everybody there. It was embarrassing,
but from the start his former colleagues treated him
well. He was a trusty. He even helped the guards out
when they were short-handed. Sure, he was a murderer
by his own admission, but in some ways he was still one
of them. Maybe they thought: there but for the grace
of God go I. A lot of guys have a gun, a mistress, and
a short temper.

I couldn't help feeling sorry for him myself. Sure it
was a horrible crime—not only shooting Joy Robinson
but her daughter, too. But the thing was, Herb Glover
was really a nice guy, a basically decent guy.

I got Wilbur Davis, the investigator I use most frequently, appointed by the court to see if he could come
up with any background that might help Herb, anything
at all. And Wilbur is a hell of a detective, a real miracle
worker.

He is a former Philadelphia police homicide detective

who went into business on his own to make more money. Because he is black, he can find out things in a black neighborhood no white detective would ever learn. And he is effective in most white situations as well. However, if Wilbur feels that his race will prevent him from getting all the information necessary in a case, he just assigns one of his white operatives to the case.

In this case Wilbur Davis came up with a miracle. It turned out that one time when Joy was fighting with her second husband, she'd taken a shot at him. She missed. If she hadn't, Herb Glover would have avoided an awful lot of trouble. Anyway, it can help a gun-owner to show that the person he shot was a shooter.

Naturally, we lined up character witnesses. We could have had them by the dozen, even a state representative and law-enforcement officers.

I got the court to appoint a psychiatrist, who examined Herb Glover and issued a beaut of a report. It talked about how the defendant felt trapped and confused, propelled helplessly toward the destruction of a marriage he'd begun to cherish more and more, filled with dread when the victim had picked up the telephone. His reasoning was warped by the heat of passion, his judgment was impaired. (It is not a bad thing at a time like this to find a male-chauvinist psychiatrist.)

All I was aiming for, all I *could* aim for, was to get the charge reduced from first degree—which would mean a life sentence—to murder two, or if wildly lucky, voluntary manslaughter.

My argument for voluntary manslaughter was novel, at least. One element needed to establish this degree is "legal provocation." Somebody calling you a name is not

legal provocation—mere words are never enough—but if
you come home and find your spouse in bed with another,
that's legal provocation.

(In fact, in Texas a husband who shoots a wife
found with a lover is committing *excusable* homicide.)

I decided to argue that what Joy had attempted to do
was similar to a lover going to bed with a spouse. Even
though my client was the one having an extramarital
relationship, it was Joy who had threatened to break up
his marriage.

It was on that shaky foundation that I hoped to establish a defense.

But this was a case where the argument that really
counted was not in front of a judge or a jury, but in front
of the chief of homicide in the DA's office. I had gathered up all this evidence to try to convince him that he
was facing a long and difficult trial; that it wasn't going
to be open and shut for murder one. I was going to pa-
rade in my psychiatrist, my detective, all my witnesses.
And I recognized that he had a terrific backlog—so
maybe we could make a deal.

I think maybe I got a good reception from the chief,
Joe McLaughlin, because he knew and liked Herb
Glover. In fact, if not for his position, he'd probably
have been another character witness.

Anyway, he agreed to negotiate, and we were at it for
days. We agreed to plead guilty to murder in the second
degree and accept a maximum sentence of ten to twenty
years if he would agree to drop the charge of murder in
the first degree as well as all charges relating to the
shooting of the daughter. After we agreed, we had to
find a judge willing to accept our agreement.

That took some searching; but finally one was found.

(Defense attorneys are not the only ones who judge-shop —DAs judge-shop too.)

Glover got full credit for the time he'd already been in jail and under the prerelease and furlough program, he can be out after putting in only five years.

I thought this was a fantastic victory, but Glover wasn't all that happy. He has seen guys with two- and three-page criminal records get five-to-ten-year sentences, so naturally he thought that he ought to do better.

Glover has known a lot of bad guys as a prison guard and as a sheriff; and as remorseful as he is about what he's done, it's tough for him to see himself as a bad guy. He isn't a real bad guy, either . . . he just had a gun in his hand at the wrong time.

12

Women Clients

Women are a rarity in criminal court, although they seem to be appearing more and more. I mean as defendants, of course, not as victims or witnesses. For every thirty male clients I defend, I have only one female client. And that one will more often than not be involved in a minor charge—prostitution, shoplifting, a drug bust, or a liquor violation.

Some of my clients are girlfriends of dope pushers or users who have been shoved around and used by their men. The practice is for a guy dealing in drugs to go with a girl who is "clean," who has no record. When he gets drugs, he stashes them on the girl, in her pocket or pocketbook. Then if they get busted, she has the stuff. The cops may realize it's really his, but they can't prove it. So she goes to court. He'll pay for the lawyer, of course, and he knows a first offender won't get worse than probation. But after she takes the rap, that's the end of their affair. He wants a new girl who has no record.

If the charge is major where a woman is concerned, then it is probably murder. And the victim was probably the defendant's husband or boyfriend. That's just the way it is. Actually, the majority of murders in this country are intrafamily (or intralover) affairs.

As many wives kill their husbands as husbands kill their wives: men tend to use guns, women to use knives.

There is a tendency among judges to go easy on women defendants; maybe it's an old-fashioned reluctance to believe women can do terrible things. So a woman has a good chance to get a break in court.

Under the common law, there is even a defense called "coverture," which says that if a married couple commits a crime, the presumption is that the husband did it and forced his spouse to cooperate. Coverture is still part of the law, but in this liberated era is less likely to be heeded.

A woman is less likely than a man to be sentenced to jail, but if once sentenced, she is often dealt with more harshly—*except* in the cases of spouse-murder. There, statistics show, women do get shorter sentences than men.

I thought I had done pretty well one time when I got ten years' probation for a man who shot his wife. But I did even better for Mary Dayson, who stabbed her husband. She got only five years' probation.

Husband-wife killings are known in the vernacular as "Mom and Pop" cases. The classic "Mom and Pop" case starts with a quarrel and ends with a corpse. Mary Dayson's case was just like that.

Mary Dayson was a forty-five-year-old woman who worked as a nurse's aide in a hospital. She'd been married and divorced while still a very young girl. She had a daughter who had four children of her own. When Mary Dayson was thirty-five, she took up with Edgar Abbott, who is best described as her second husband, even though that isn't legally accurate.

Edgar Abbott and Mary Dayson lived together as man and wife, but they didn't actually get married. That was because Edgar already had a wife, and five children, too, living a few blocks away. Every once in a while, Edgar Abbott would go home to his legal wife, siring a child while there, and then come back to take up domestic bliss once again with Mary.

Mary outweighed Edgar by about sixty pounds and topped him in height by a good three inches. He was a skinny five feet eight; she was a hefty almost six feet.

Mary and Edgar got along fine for most of those ten years, but things had been going sour in the twelve months before the tragedy. Edgar was always a drinker; he used to get drunk once a week. And he was really a sweet guy except when he was drinking.

But in those twelve months, he was drinking even more, getting drunk once a day. He was, in fact, a fargone alcoholic. The autopsy showed his liquor content was enough to kill a social drinker. But it wasn't booze that finished Edgar off; it was a stab wound.

One fateful fall Sunday evening in 1973, Mary and her sister Ellen came together to Mary's house. (Incidentally, Mary owned the house.) They had spent the day together, first going to church, then visiting Mary's daughter and grandchildren, then having dinner with Mary's (and Ellen's) mother.

When Mary got home, Edgar was upstairs, drunk. That wasn't unexpected. But he was also naked and sitting on the bed with a young neighbor named Steven, who was a homosexual. Mary lost her temper. Get out, she told Steve, who went. It wasn't that Mary didn't like Steve. She did. She'd known him since he was a little boy. And it wasn't that she was affronted by his homosexuality. She didn't give a damn. She just didn't want him doing his thing with Edgar in the master bedroom.

Mary sent a few parting remarks at Edgar and went downstairs to have a few drinks with her sister. Edgar came downstairs and a real rouser of a quarrel started. Mary won that round. Edgar fell into the TV set and cut the corner of his eye. He went upstairs to repair the damage.

Mary continued to drink. Edgar was a real drunk, but Mary had a drinking problem, too. She invited the ousted Steve to come back and join her. Then she went upstairs to go to the bathroom.

Before getting to the bathroom, she passed the bedroom and unfortunately couldn't resist picking up the fight with Edgar once more. She told him to get out. She told him she couldn't take his behavior any more. He was rubbing his cut eye with a towel. "See where drinking gets you," she rebuked him.

The battle moved from the verbal to the physical. Then Mary saw that Edgar had something in his hand. She said she thought it was a fingernail file. She grabbed for it, got it away from him, and stabbed him with it. It wasn't a fingernail file . . . it was a paring knife.

Edgar staggered and fell into a chair. Mary thought he'd suffered a seizure. She yelled for help and began giving him artificial respiration. Steve tried to help, too. Ellen called the police rescue squad.

Then Mary saw the wound in Edgar's chest and she knew what she had done. She washed off the knife, changed her robe. She told both Steve and her sister to tell the police Edgar had been hurt outside—mugged—and they agreed. The sister did indeed tell that story. But Steve told of hearing the quarreling from downstairs and going up to see if he could help.

He saw Mary—who, you recall, was bigger than her husband—toss Edgar off the bed and yell at him to get out. Mary herself told the police that she had stabbed Edgar and also that she had asked her sister and Steve to lie.

The upshot was that Mary was arrested. She wasn't taken right to jail, but to a hospital. (Mary suffered from angina, hypertension, and asthma, all conditions that are aggravated by tension. And Mary was tense enough to be plenty sick.)

It wasn't until the next day, then, that Mary's mother and daughter showed up in my office to ask me to take her case. Unfortunately, that was too late for me to have prevented Mary from making any statement. The women had been referred to me by a local judge who knew the Dayson family for twenty years.

The obvious excuse for such a crime is self-defense. "He came at me with a knife . . . I feared for my life. . . . There wasn't anything else I could do."

However, self-defense isn't as easy to prove as many people think. First off, you have to show that you tried to retreat before resorting to violence, or that you had no opportunity to retreat. ("My back was up against the wall. . . .")

There are rules that govern who has the obligation to retreat in various situations. For example, if you are in somebody else's house and that somebody threatens you,

you are supposed to try to leave before taking stronger measures.

However, if that somebody else threatens you and you are in *your* house, he's the one with the obligation to leave. If you order him to go and he doesn't, you are entitled to use some force to oust him. If he fights back, you can fight back harder.

The situation was not clear in Mary Dayson's situation. Sure, it was her house. She owned it. And legally speaking, Edgar was not her husband. But the fact that he'd lived there for ten years gave him resident status. Neither Mary nor Edgar was obliged to leave the house; however, *both* were under the obligation of attempting to physically separate rather than come to blows.

True, Mary had said that Edgar came after her with a weapon—the "fingernail file" that turned out to be a knife—and that she'd grabbed it to save herself. But it was Mary who pursued the quarrel, it was Mary who was bigger, and, according to Steve's story, it was Mary who first bounced Edgar off the bed. Who told Mary to go upstairs anyway? Why didn't she just continue to the bathroom and let things cool off? The DA was sure to concentrate on these aspects.

What Mary did have going for her was the fact that there was only one stab wound. She grabbed the knife from him and stabbed to get him away: she didn't repeatedly attack him. She did try to revive him afterward. She did ask Ellen to call for help.

The DA would point out that Mary coolly thought of making up a story about a mugging. I would point out that Mary didn't resort to telling that story when arrested.

You may wonder whether it is a disadvantage to a defense attorney to have as a client somebody whose life-style is not that of the average judge. Will the judge hold it against the defendant that she drinks, that she lives in sin, that she is friendly with a homosexual, etc.?

The answer to that is no, not if the judge is an urban realist with some trial experience. Sure, maybe some civil-court judge or newcomer to the bench might not understand. But an experienced criminal-court judge doesn't judge lifestyles, just the evidence in the case. Did Mary stab Edgar in self-defense or did she stab him in the heat of passion or did she do it in cold premeditation?

I really didn't want to go to a jury trial with Mary Dayson's case. I've said before that a trial by jury is a gamble and I didn't want to gamble if I could avoid it. And while I was busy trying to avoid it, I wanted to be sure Mary was out on bail. That wasn't just because it would be easier on her—and on me—to have her out. It was also because I wanted her to go back to her job so that later I could argue before a judge (or a jury, if necessary) that this hard-working woman had been accepted back by her co-workers, that they were willing to continue to work with her despite what had happened. By dint of arguing with the DA's office and pleading with a judge, I got bail set at eight thousand dollars. Mary's family could get up 10 percent of that to get her out. At the preliminary hearing, I fought to get the charge reduced from murder to voluntary or even involuntary manslaughter. (Of course, I also stressed self-defense, hoping to end the case right there.) But the best I could manage was to convince the judge to add as alternatives both involuntary and voluntary manslaughter to the murder charge, so that these, too, could later be decided by a judge or jury.

I went to talk to Joe McLaughlin, the chief of homicide for the DA's office in 1974. We had just had an election in Philadelphia and the new district attorney had pledged to cut the backlog in homicide cases. The word was out that McLaughlin was Santa Claus. If a defense attorney made him a reasonable offer to avoid a trial, one could probably work out a good deal. I came in with five cases at once. I was ready to deal wholesale, and, frankly, it is usually easier to get a good bargain when you are talking about lowering the backlog by five instead of one. I did get deals on four, of which Mary Dayson's case was one. The other I finally had to take to trial.

I wanted as much evidence on hand to convince McLaughlin as I would have wanted to convince a judge. Wilbur Davis found out for me that Edgar Abbott, the sweet guy who only got nasty when he was drunk, got *very* nasty when drunk. He'd once stabbed his sister-in-law in the face and once disarmed a policeman who had stopped him and turned the cop's own gun on him. He missed, however.

I talked it up to Joe about how big a case I could make out of this, how good this woman was. She had raised a daughter. She worked hard every day. She owned her home. She helped with her grandchildren. She was good to her mother. And she was only defending herself. McLaughlin countered with that statement from Steve, with the basic logic that Mary didn't have to put herself in that room with Edgar.

Finally, though, we came to an agreement. He agreed that the charge would not rise above voluntary manslaughter, and, at my request, he even wrote that in red ink on the front of his file. On my side, I agreed that we would waive a jury trial—if the case could be heard by Judge Juanita Kidd Stout. I figured Judge Stout might accept our argument of self-defense, but failing that, she probably wouldn't send a good mother and a hard worker away to jail.

When we came before the judge, the DA first asked for a postponement. It seems that the major prosecution witness, Steve the neighbor, had disappeared. That might well have been because Wilbur Davis explained to Steve that if he hadn't yet been served with a subpoena (and at the time Davis saw Steve he had not been), then he couldn't be forced to come to court. Obviously Steve had to decide whether he wanted to help convict Mary of Edgar's death or not. He had been friendly with both of them. If he testified against Mary, they wouldn't stay friends long. Edgar, of course, was in no condition to be friends with anybody. Steve apparently decided to help Mary, and I can't say I was unhappy when I didn't see Steve in the courtroom.

Judge Stout had lots of cases in front of her and she wasn't disposed to delay—she ordered the assistant DA who had been assigned the case to proceed. All other witnesses were on hand. The DA had brought Edgar's legal family to the courtroom.

They were definitely on the prosecution's side. Edgar may have been an indifferent husband and father, but they were willing to forgive him and not willing to forgive Mary.

The assistant DA wanted to push for murder. I had to push back and said that his chief had agreed to a deal. Judge Stout sent him out of the courtroom to confirm that such a deal had been made. And of course it had. The judge found Mary guilty of voluntary manslaughter and deferred sentence until the probation office submitted its report.

Sentencing took place late in the afternoon a few weeks later. Judge Stout had presided for the previous week over a jury trial in which the defendant was accused of being part of a gang rape and murder. A young couple had been overpowered outside a museum. The girl was raped, the boy was drowned in a fountain. Just before we came in for the Dayson sentencing, that jury reported itself deadlocked. Judge Stout sent them back to think about the evidence some more.

I can't help but think that the judge had to be struck by the contrast in the two cases. One a vicious murder, totally unprovoked, unreasoning; the other, a tragic mess-up between lovers. The probation department had stressed the kind of woman Mary was: good mother, a hard worker. I naturally had stressed the kind of man Edgar was: an absent father, a hard drinker.

Mary looked pitiful in the courtroom. She had been depressed since the crime and had moved in with her mother to avoid the memories that would always be in the house she shared with Edgar. She was still sick, and obviously prison would make her sicker.

And Judge Stout, as I previously indicated, sentenced her to only five years' probation. I don't think the fact that the defendant was a woman was the prime reason for that sentence, but, then, I don't think it hurt either.

13

Rape Victims

The least-reported major crime in the United States is rape. And women, who have been speaking up more and more on the subject, claim the reason it isn't much reported is that rape is the only crime in which the victim gets treated more like a criminal than the criminal.

The women point out that when a man is robbed of twenty-five dollars, no defense attorney accuses him of "enticing" the robber by owning a wallet or implies he wasn't "really robbed" because he's been known to *give away* money in the past. The women complain—with justification—that when they take the witness stand, the defense attorney will try to make a judge or jury believe they "asked for it," "consented to it," or aren't very moral anyway.

I tried hard to win rape cases when I was an assistant DA, and I concede they are among the hardest of all cases to win.

Take the case of Ann Fleming, a twenty-six-year-old

airline stewardess who had been invited to a party. She went with another woman, a cousin.

When the party ended, one of the guests, Fred Lyman, thirty-six, offered to drive the two young women and two other men to their homes. They all gratefully accepted the lift. The cousin was dropped off first, then the two men were dropped off, but Fred Lyman took Ann Fleming to his apartment, where he first raped her and then forced her to pose in erotic positions in the nude, while he took photographs.

"These pictures," Lyman told Ann, "are my insurance that you won't go to the police."

Lyman recognized, of course, that as humiliated as a woman must feel testifying about a sexual assault of any kind, she must feel doubly humiliated to know that the police would find nude photographs of her.

But when Lyman finally released her at 7:00 A.M., Ann Fleming went first to a hospital and then to a police station. The police drove her around the neighborhood where she said she'd been taken. She spotted Lyman on the street, and he was promptly arrested.

And, of course, Lyman produced the photographs. His story was that he was a free-lance photographer (and in fact he was), that Ann Fleming had agreed to pose for him. Her problem, he said, was that she was mad because he'd only paid her fifteen dollars and she wanted thirty. She was just a greedy broad trying to make trouble for poor old Fred.

Ann Fleming had to watch those nude photos of herself passed from hand to hand and marked "Exhibit A." Lyman's defense attorney pointed out that Ann's expression in those photos was perfectly bland—she was not crying, she did not appear to be in pain.

Ann said the expression wasn't bland; it was numb.

At this point, all you have for a case is one person's word against the other's.

Luckily for Ann Fleming and unluckily for Fred Lyman, the police were able to get additional evidence. It seems that Ann Fleming had not been Fred's first victim. The police got a warrant to search his apartment and uncovered other photographs of nude women in erotic poses. The police were either unable to identify the women or could not, understandably, persuade them to come forward and identify the photos in open court. However, the photographs alone told the story of Fred Lyman. Maybe Ann Fleming's expression was "bland" or "numb," but the expressions of the other women ran the gamut of horror. There were tears, there were terrible grimaces, there were painful contortions.

Fred Lyman was convicted. If not for those other photos, though, I'm not sure that would have been the result.

The toughest rape case I ever prosecuted was a vicious gang rape that the police actually broke up while it was in progress.

You'd think that one would be a snap to win . . . but not with rape.

Shortly after midnight on Easter Sunday 1968, three young women and their dates were in the apartment of one of them, enjoying a party, when the door burst open and a gang of about twenty men rushed in. They broke a lamp, overpowered the girls' dates with knives and fists, and proceeded to strip the three girls and rape them—repeatedly.

Two of the three girls admittedly had less than virginal

reputations. But the third, a beautiful girl, whom many men had asked out and had been turned down, was considered not only a "nice girl" but "standoffish." And it was this girl who seemed to be the primary target of the rapists. She was spread-eagled on a bed and raped at least a dozen times. The expression is "pulling a train": one after the other, after the other.

It went on for more than an hour. And then a girl who lived in another apartment in this house went by the door, looked in, and saw and heard what was going on. She ran to the police station, which was located only a half-block away.

The police came en masse, and suddenly there were men coming out of the apartment every which way. They went out the windows, the front door, the side door. The cops were picking them up as they emerged.

One man was grabbed inside as he was pulling his pants up. Another was literally plucked off the girl on the bed. Another was pulled out from under the bed.

There must have been twenty of them, all told, but we felt we really only had evidence against seven of them. And we went to trial against five of those seven at once. (The other two were tried separately because their attorneys were not available for trial when the attorneys for the five could be assembled. It was tough enough getting five lawyers together at one time, so we moved ahead.)

This case took six weeks to try: two weeks just to pick a jury. It took one hundred and eighty prospective jurors to select twelve jurors and two alternates because there was the entire battery of defense attorneys questioning and challenging in addition to the DA, who could also question and challenge. The defense will challenge anybody who says he might believe the word of a police officer over that of an ordinary citizen (because police testimony was going to be crucial in this case) and the DA didn't want anybody who thinks three girls who go to a party with three boys are "asking for trouble."

The defense claimed, of course, that this was no rape, this was a party . . . giving the distinct impression that everybody knew in advance that an orgy was planned. The defense made a big thing out of the fact that the girls were not screaming for help.

They implied that if the neighbor had been able to go for help, the three girls would have been equally free to leave the building if they had wanted to.

And friends of the men testified that they knew about the party—it was all just great fun.

We countered that the gang of rapists were uninvited guests to this "party," that girls facing twenty guys with knives may be afraid to scream, and that the neighbor probably got away only because she was unnoticed.

The defense claimed that even if the girls were attacked, they could not identify the specific defendants as their attackers. The men had extinguished all light when they broke the lamp. It was pitch-dark, so how could the victims see anyone?

The beautiful girl who had suffered the most testified that street light filtered in through one of the windows, that even the moon shed some light, and that further, the men were smoking and when one would light a match, she could see his face.

The defense rebutted this by pointing out that this girl had identified someone at the preliminary hearing who turned out to have an iron-clad alibi. So obviously, this was a young woman who could make a mistake, whose identifications were not reliable.

It really began to look as if this case was going to be lost. In fact, I was given the authorization to offer probation if anybody cared to plead guilty and save us the expense of a long trial. But nobody pleaded guilty; they were all very confident of getting off.

At one point, the defense contended that a police witness had to be lying because he said he went out the bathroom window in pursuit of one of the defendants, and obviously nobody could go through such a window. Well, we went to the house, removed the entire window, and brought it into court to show that this policeman could go through it. But the judge wouldn't let me put it before the jury—too prejudicial, he said.

And then I wanted to argue that if this was just a friendly orgy with everybody so willing, why did all the guys jump out the windows when the police arrived? But the judge wouldn't allow that either—too prejudicial.

The defense brought out that one of the girls had a half-sister who was a prostitute. The defense brought out inconsistencies in the girls' testimony: one had said she and another of the girls had stopped at a hairdresser's shop that day, the other girl said they hadn't.

Whether or not they went to have their hair done had nothing to do with whether or not they were raped, but a lot to do with their credibility. If they would lie about a hairdresser, would they lie about a rape?

Now, as it turned out, all five defendants in this case were convicted. And I think there were just three reasons why that happened.

First, there was the appearance and virtuous reputation of the girl who had been spread-eagled on the bed. Around city hall they began calling her the "Virgin Queen." The defense was never able to show that she was sexually experienced. She was a very sympathetic witness.

Second, the defense had made a big thing out of the fact that medical records from the hospital to which the girls had been taken by police showed no evidence of spermatozoa in smears taken from the Virgin Queen.

Now, I just couldn't believe that. I couldn't believe that at least twelve guys had raped this girl and not one of them had left one little sperm behind. And I knew damn well the jury wouldn't be able to believe that either. So I just called in medical experts to reexamine the slides under a microscope right in the courtroom—and they found the medical records were in error; there were spermatozoa aplenty in the smears.

And third, the defense did not put one of the defendants on the stand. That, of course, saved any of the defendants from having to answer any questions about his previous sexual—or maybe criminal—past. And no doubt the defense felt they'd thrown up enough doubt that an acquittal was sure. Sometimes just attacking the prosecution's case is really all a defense attorney can do, anyway.

But in this particular trial, not putting a defendant on the stand was a mistake. The jury had seen these young girls on the stand for two of the six weeks: they had been mercilessly cross-examined on the most intimate details. They had been practically undressed in front of the jury, you might say. And here these men weren't even willing to get up there and deny the crime? I think it had to strike the jurors as unfair. In fact, when the defense rested, not putting a defendant on the stand, I looked over at the jury foreman. And his mouth literally dropped open. I could tell he was shocked at that. And I looked at the jury and shrugged, as if to say, "See what kind of guys these are?" I don't know if the jury got the full meaning of my shrug, but they did convict.

The judge then passed out sentences ranging from one to eight years to five to fifteen years, and even as he did that, he commented that, after all, these girls had gone there to a party . . . they probably had immoral plans.

I have noticed a decrease in that kind of remark lately as we have gotten more female judges on the bench. But many male judges really hate to dump on a guy for rape.

I prosecuted a man who was known among police and members of the DA's staff as the "Phantom Fucker." The newspapers referred to him more delicately as the "Masked Rapist."

This man would break into homes during the day when a housewife and her children would be there alone, and he would always wear a mask.

He'd rob the home and rape the housewife. And even though the women would report the crime, they could never describe what this man looked like. There were no clues.

But one time the Phantom Fucker enjoyed a rapee so much, he promised her he'd be back. When she told that to the police, they staked out her place with a police-woman and a stakeout squad. They waited there for a week, and then watched as a man wearing a mask broke into the house and began dragging the housewife off to the bedroom. The police moved in, shot him in the rear end, and removed his mask from his other end.

We placed twenty-eight charges against this guy and

announced that the Phantom Fucker was through. Admittedly, we would have trouble proving all twenty-eight, but there was no doubt about the fact that he'd been caught burglarizing one home and attacking one woman. We negotiated a deal with his attorney; he agreed to plead guilty in return for a ten-to-forty-year jail sentence.

And the judge reduced the sentence to five to fifteen. He said the man had an excellent employment record; that he was a good and kind person, a devoted family man.

Sure he was good and kind—all he did was rape women.

Legally a woman is raped if she says no and the man proceeds as if she has said yes. This is supposed to apply even if the woman knows the rapist, even if she has dated him, even if she once slept with him. That may be the law, but that isn't how the average jury sees it.

As a DA, I lost a case in which a young coed, the virginal daughter of a police official, was raped by her boyfriend. She was a very proper young lady and she had never gone to bed with this young man. But she would invite him over to watch television with her. And she was comfortable enough with him so that she'd change into a nightgown and a robe while he was still there. She'd go into the bedroom and change and then come out, sit down next to him, and continue to watch TV.

On one particular night, the boyfriend forced his attentions upon her. Outraged, she charged him with rape.

But obviously the jury didn't see it that way. Apparently the jury felt that she had "led him on" by changing out of her clothes into a nightgown. And after all, he wasn't some stranger who had bopped her on the head and dragged her into an alley.

I know the fact that a woman's morals or appearance are questioned in relation to whether or not a man did or did not take sexual advantage of her strikes women as absurd, but it is a very common defense in rape cases.

Now, while I was a DA, I became very sympathetic to women and understood why they resented the shabby way defense attorneys treated them. However, when I became a defense attorney, I treated them the same way. If I am paid to defend, I will defend. And an acceptable defense in a rape case is to question the woman's morals.

One of the first cases I handled after leaving the DA's office was a rape case.

It seems that when I was a DA and prosecuting a murder case, a local high school senior class visited the courtroom to observe "justice in action." That happens all the time. Well, one of the girls in the class apparently remembered my name and when I set up practice for myself she called me and asked me to represent her brother.

She said he was charged with rape and kidnapping. The first thing I did was to arrange for her brother to surrender. I sent my investigator, Wilbur Davis, to go with him to the police and tell him not to make any statements. And Wilbur hung around the station until the kid was transferred out of the district just to make sure that the arresting officers could not later claim that they'd been talking to my client, who said "she was a real good fuck" or something like that.

I didn't get to meet my client until the bail hearing. He was nineteen and wild-looking . . . really wild. He had long hair and his nickname was "Ramrod." Great!

Ramrod told me, and later testified, that he and another boy did pick this girl up in a playground; she was fourteen but looked seventeen. They rode around; they went swimming; they went to his father's garage and just "messed around some"—nothing serious, you understand. And everything they did was "consensual."

I knew that if Ramrod was found guilty of actually having intercourse with this girl, the fact that we might prove it "consensual" would be immaterial. A fourteen-year-old is not allowed to consent to intercourse. It is still statutory rape even if she attacks the guy first.

The preliminary hearing took place in front of a judge who has five daughters—not much opportunity to maneuver there. The trial took place in front of a judge who was a bachelor—much more hopeful.

It developed that this girl came from a very well-to-do family and had a very strict upbringing. When she came to that playground, which was in a working-class area, she was really slumming. Maybe she was looking for adventure. Maybe she was lonely. Who knows?

She meets the boys—Ramrod and his pal—and she agrees to go with them. The pal's family has a swimming pool and they decide to go skinny-dipping. Now maybe she didn't want to . . . maybe she just didn't know how to say no . . . but she did that. Then she gets back in the car and they drive to this garage and "fool around." Was it consensual or was she just scared—not knowing how to handle these two boys?

The boys then take her back to the playground. She tells a friend there that she was raped, and then she gets back in the car and the boys take her home. If she was raped, why get back in the car? Maybe she just didn't know what else to do. Maybe she was afraid.

What you believe depends on whether you believe the prosecution or the defense. She didn't tell her mother about being with the boys until the next day. Her mother took her to the hospital and the hospital found she had a ripped hymen and a swollen vulva.

My client who, when he was with me, had looked like a teenaged dirty old man, looked like the All-American Boy in court. I got him cleaned up and made him wear a sports jacket.

And we introduced witnesses, found by Wilbur at the playground, who testified that they knew this girl and had necked with her. One of them looked even worse than my client when my client looked his worst. The implication was: look what kind of guy this girl will neck with.

We went after the medical testimony because she hadn't gone to the hospital until twenty-one hours after the alleged event. Who knows what can happen in twenty-one hours? Maybe she went out with some other guys.

And when this girl took the stand, I cross-examined the hell out of her. When I finished she was hysterical. I got her to admit to taking drugs. I got her to admit she'd lied to her mother about what had happened . . . she'd originally told her mother she was forced to go with the boys. She even said the boys had not penetrated her.

It was understandable that the girl would lie to her mother, who was very strict. And it wasn't really relevant that she took drugs. But it clouds the issue. It attacks her character.

The judge was left with a mess. He couldn't convict my client of statutory rape if there was no rape. And if it were a sexual assault (if they put their fingers in her vagina, for instance, while "fooling around"), the issue of consent and character became critical.

And so both boys—my client and his pal—were acquitted. The girl was weeping; the boys were smiling. I had the feeling that the girl may not have been raped, but had been taken advantage of anyway. Still, she wasn't my client.

Just because I think that women often get the short end in rape cases doesn't mean I think women are always right and the men are always wrong. Sometimes the man really is the victim of a woman instead of the other way round.

Like Vincent Morris and Alan Raymond. Morris was my client first. A relative of his called me one day asking me to represent him because he had been shot in the stomach and was in the hospital. I offered my sympathies, of course, but I said I couldn't see why he needed representing, if he was the victim.

It turned out he was the victim of a boyfriend who claimed Morris and Raymond had raped his girlfriend. The boyfriend tracked the two down to the local YMCA swimming pool and started shooting. Police were guarding the hospital room.

The first thing I suggested was that they bring me a cash retainer. It was then dinner time and I'd have to get clearance from police headquarters to go to the hospital to see the prisoner and, what the hell, if he was in the hospital, bail wouldn't help.

However, I said if they came with the cash, I'd go see what I could do. They came, and I went.

I found out that Morris and Raymond were charged with rape, corrupting the morals of a minor, conspiracy to help lesbians commit sodomy, and a few other things. The woman in the case was seventeen years old: tiny, big-eyed, and pretty. The defendants in the case were both twenty-four, more than six feet tall, and husky. It did not look good.

When I went to see Morris, I found Raymond lying on the next bed and he hired me too. The courts are very touchy about one lawyer representing two codefendants. It might be in the interest of one to make a deal by testifying against the other. But neither of these men wanted a deal; they said they were innocent.

Morris said he had known the young lady in the case, whose name was Linda, for a good long while. In fact, he'd sold her his old car. He'd asked six hundred dollars for it but Linda didn't have that much so she suggested he might want to bring down the price if she spent some time with him in a downtown motel. She spent a lot of time with him and the car price kept going down.

Linda did not tell her boyfriend about all of this, of course. He was a possessive, overbearing type, who slapped her if he even caught her smoking.

One day Linda came by to see Vincent Morris at the parking lot, where he was just getting off work, and his friend Alan Raymond was there. The three of them strolled together to Rittenhouse Square—a tiny enclave of lawn and park benches in the middle of the city. There they met two nineteen-year-old women Vincent knew— both college coeds and both lesbians.

Now they were five and they decided to take a drive. They got into Alan's car and headed out to Fairmount Park—a huge enclave of lawn and benches. They smoked a little pot. They talked. They parked and began having some fun and games. The girls started to undress each other. The boys got undressed too.

A police car pulled up. A park guard came over to the car to see what was going on. He saw. In fact, he decided to stick around and join in. A second patrol car came along. The patrolman radioed headquarters that he was going off duty for a while. Everybody was having relations with everybody.

Later, for some reason—maybe she was nervous that he would find out anyway—Linda told her boyfriend she'd been raped.

Accompanied by his brother, the boyfriend went gunning for Alan and Vincent at the pool. He emptied his gun. Two of the bullets went into the water, but luckily no innocent bystanders were hurt.

The police arrested the two buddies, the two brothers, the two lesbians, and the two park guards. Only two were my clients, but two of this group were enough.

At the preliminary hearing Linda came on like a demure princess. Her grandmother escorted her in. Linda minimized the behavior of the police. Well, yes, they did watch, but she didn't claim they raped her. The district attorney, however, was apparently convinced the guards did more than look.

I was thrilled that police were charged in this mess. Because I couldn't see how my guys were going to be convicted of rape if police testified that it was just a big party.

The charges were toned down somewhat at the preliminary hearing. Just corrupting the morals of a minor and rape. That's bad enough, but all the sodomy and other stuff were dropped.

We were heading for a trial, and that didn't make me happy. Because, though the story was wild, this girl looked so sweet, you couldn't tell what a jury would believe.

I was trying to talk to the brothers . . . I wanted Vincent to talk to the girl . . . maybe something could be worked out. Vince did take the girl out and ask her why she'd gotten him in all this trouble. She replied she was so terrified of her boyfriend that she'd lied and ripped her clothing to convince him. She said she wanted to tell the truth now but her grandmother wouldn't let her.

I called up the chief of major trials, Arthur Makadon, and told him he ought to get that girl to take a lie detector test.

I told him what she'd told Vince and, as an added fillip, I said Vince had gotten it all on tape.

Vince had told me he had a tape machine in his car— one that records as well as plays. I just assumed that he'd know enough to turn the damn thing on when Linda was talking. I assumed too much. It never occurred to him.

I did not feel pressed to report that to Makadon, however, especially since he'd been so impressed with this evidence I'd told him existed, he'd agreed to polygraph Linda. I kept "forgetting" to bring the tape to him.

Believe me, if I'd actually had such a tape, I wouldn't have worried about getting it to Makadon. I would have played it at a trial and made national headlines. But anyway, before Linda was even hooked up to the machine, she confessed. She had lied; she had ripped her own clothes; she hadn't been raped. She had slept with Vincent to get a car at a bargain price. She had confessed to Vincent, but she didn't think he'd taped it. (Smart girl.)

I finally had to admit to Makadon that I didn't have a tape. He was miffed but he realized that justice was done. And the next day, he appeared in court himself to move for a not guilty verdict for the friends and for the lesbians. Charges had already been thrown out against one of the park guards, but the other was dismissed from the force.

The upshot was that two friends had been shot, Vince lost the job at the parking lot he'd held for five years, the two lesbians were expelled from college, and one of the park guards lost his job. The boyfriend's brother was acquitted of all charges, but the boyfriend, who did the shooting, was sent to prison for two to seven years.

Linda? Nothing at all happened to Linda.

14

The DA's Job

Since I've been on both sides of the criminal justice system, I'd like to say something about some of the differences in role each side plays. It isn't just a matter of one side tries to convict, the other to acquit. It isn't just a matter of equal but opposite goals. Not at all.

The district attorney's job is, to quote from a Pennsylvania Supreme Court decision, "not to convict but to see justice is done." The U.S. Supreme Court has said the DA's role is not just to win conviction but to see that "criminal trials are fair."

So, you might say, in one way a DA has a terrific advantage over a poor defense lawyer. He gets to pick and choose his cases. A DA doesn't *have to* prosecute somebody just because the police have nabbed him. If the DA is convinced there really isn't a good case, he can, on his own initiative, ask for a directed verdict of "not guilty" or ask that the charges be dismissed. If the DA really thinks the cops have the wrong person, he can make a defense attorney unnecessary.

The defense attorney can't decide on his own hook to make the DA unnecessary. If the DA is going ahead, the defense attorney has no choice but to go ahead. And the defense attorney's personal convictions about the guilt or innocence of his client have absolutely no bearing on that client's right to a defense.

In another way, though, the defense attorney has a great advantage over the DA. The defense attorney's *only* job is to defend. He can attack the DA. He can call him a "persecutor, not a prosecutor." He is not required to reveal whether his client has confessed the crime to him. He is not obliged to help the DA convict his client—not in any way.

But the DA is required to help the defense acquit—if he can. The U.S. Supreme Court has said that if the DA finds evidence that might point to innocence as well as evidence that might point to guilt, both must be made public. If the DA does not plan to offer the former himself, he must turn it over to the defense attorney.

Now, whether in actual practice the DA worries about *finding* evidence of innocence as well as guilt is a debatable point. And quite frankly, the mere fact that the defense attorney sees something as "evidence of innocence" is no guarantee the DA will view it the same way.

In general, though, the prosecutor is the one who backs the police, who backs the victims of the crime. The defense attorney is the one looking for flaws in police work, the one backing the accused, innocent or guilty.

When I was in the DA's office, I was a pretty hard-nosed prosecutor. Sure, I was interested in justice, but when you are on the prosecution side, your definition of justice tends to come down a little harder on the criminals than a defense attorney's definition would.

For example, I foiled a parole for Willie Sutton—for a couple of years, anyway. He finally did get out of prison in 1970, and I was attacked by both defense attorneys and the press as an unforgiving, even vindictive, bastard. I looked at it as just doing my job.

Willie Sutton—also known nationally as "Slick Willie" or "Willie the Actor"—was equally adept at robbing banks and escaping from jail. Willie is probably one of the last of the old-style hoods still in existence. In his day, he was pretty famous. ("Why do you rob banks?" a judge once asked Willie. "Because that's where the money is," he replied.)

Willie went to jail for the first time in the twenties— sentenced to five to ten in Sing Sing—for an attempted bank robbery that failed. He drew a thirty-year sentence for his second bank robbery (it succeeded but an accomplice turned him in) and escaped after only a few weeks. He sawed through bars, picked locks, got into a car a friend had thoughtfully parked near the prison, and drove away. He robbed more banks, transferring his attentions from New York to Pennsylvania. He was arrested again (another accomplice finked) and sentenced to twenty-five to fifty years in Eastern Penitentiary.

After eleven years he and a dozen other inmates dug a ninety-foot tunnel and got out. Caught again, he was put in Holmesburg, a veritable fortress.

"I won't be here long," Sutton said. And he wasn't. He was gone in a matter of months.

That was in 1947. Sutton returned to New York, worked a few years as an attendant in a nursing home, then returned to bank robbing. In 1952 a twenty-four-year-old pants presser named Arnold Schuster spotted Willie on a Brooklyn subway train. Willie's face was pretty well known. Schuster followed the "Actor" and told police where he could be found. Willie was arrested and returned to jail.

The police officers took credit for the capture and were instantly promoted by an elated police commissioner. But Schuster was irked at the police, stepped forward, and announced that he was the one who'd found Willie.

That was a mistake. Twenty days later, Schuster was found in an alley, shot to death. Bullets had been fired into his eyes, head, and stomach. Willie denied all knowledge of the crime. And in 1963, eleven years later, Cosa Nostra songbird Joe Valachi claimed Willie wasn't lying. He said that the late mob boss Albert Anastasia saw Schuster on television, said "I hate squealers," and told his gunmen to "get him." Valachi claimed that Frederick Tenuto, a Philadelphia murderer who had escaped with Willie from Holmesburg, was the triggerman. Valachi said Anastasia then had Tenuto killed to ensure his silence.

Maybe Schuster's death happened just like Valachi said it happened and maybe Sutton had nothing to do with it. On the other hand, when the police arrested Willie in 1952, he was carrying a machine gun. What the hell was this nice bank robber who claimed he really abhorred violence doing with a machine gun?

Let's just say I wasn't as sympathetic to Willie Sutton as some others were.

I became involved in the case of Willie Sutton in 1968 when he applied for a parole in New York State. He was then sixty-seven years old and he'd been sick for many years. The man had spent thirty-four of those sixty-seven years behind bars. There was a hitch in his plans for parole and that was a detainer that was lodged against him by Pennsylvania. When Willie skipped Holmesburg, he was charged with prison breach, and whenever New York released him, he would have to be brought to Philadelphia to face that charge.

So Willie's attorneys attempted to get parole for him in New York and get that Pennsylvania detainer eliminated so that Willie could just get out and go free. I fought to maintain the detainer and won.

Willie's attorneys went to federal court in New York to claim his civil rights had been violated because he hadn't had a speedy trial on the prison breach charge.

I countered with a brief that said if Willie wanted to file suit against Pennsylvania, he'd have to do it in Pennsylvania.

His attorneys said he was sick, he was dying. I said bring him to Pennsylvania and if our doctors say he's dying we'll forget the whole thing. His attorneys said that Philadelphia justice "stinks." I decried the spectacle of a man who had a life history of violating the law trying to make use of the law to avoid his obligation. (That is definitely a prosecutor-type statement.) I said Willie had once escaped through manholes, now he wanted to escape through loopholes, but the law must be served.

His attorneys said that all Willie wanted to do was get out and work with juvenile delinquents in New York. (And when he did get out, he tipped his hat to the delinquents and went to Florida to live with his sister.)

Anyway, Willie didn't get his parole in 1968. In 1970, after I'd left the DA's office, there was an agreement to drop charges, and at age sixty-nine, Sutton was free.

Was I an unforgiving, even vindictive, bastard? Maybe

so. But the point is that as a prosecutor I took the same position I do as a defense attorney—win. Go for the most you can get, not the least.

When I was in the DA's office, I negotiated with defense attorneys for sentences to avoid trials, to cut the backlog, to keep the costs down, and to get the best I could in the shortest time, just as the DAs do with me now.

I didn't win every case as a prosecutor. Sometimes those damn defense attorneys did to me what I try my best to do to the current bunch in the DA's office. They would convince a judge or jury that I hadn't managed to prove my case beyond a reasonable doubt.

Robert Williams, now a judge, ruined my record of winning murder cases by getting an acquittal for a policeman for whom I'll invent the name Harry Bartlett.

Bartlett was accused of gunning down a not-too-bright, twenty-seven-year-old, part-time handyman I'll call Stephen Manning outside a neighborhood taproom. Manning had been seen flashing a wad of bills inside the bar. His mother said he'd saved up five hundred dollars from his job. We figured it more likely he'd saved up five hundred dollars from various burglary expeditions. Anyway, Manning was found full of holes in an alley. The wad of bills was gone.

When the police arrived, they naturally questioned everybody in the area, and one of the people in the area was Harry Bartlett, who identified himself as an off-duty policeman. He said he'd been in the bar and when he heard the shots he came running out.

The homicide boys thanked him for his interest and then, just as a matter of standard procedure, asked him if he was carrying a gun on him. Actually, it was reasonable to assume he was. Most policemen carry their weapon at all times—they never know when they'll be needed in an emergency. And when Bartlett produced his gun, the homicide boys sent it over to ballistics to be checked out—just ordinary procedure.

And lo, ballistics claimed that the bullets found in the dead man's body came from this gun.

It seems the bullets contained cross hairs indicating that. Also, the bullets were a type called "wadcutters," customarily used at police pistol-practice ranges. (They make a bigger hole than an ordinary bullet, which makes them easier to see on the targets.) Bartlett had recently been at the pistol range.

On the basis of this evidence, Bartlett was arrested, indicted, and committed to prison without bail. In fact, he spent thirteen months in prison.

And through it all, he maintained his innocence, and a lot of people were on his side. Bartlett was a chunky, sunny-faced, thirty-five-year-old with a photogenic wife, two little kids, three otherwise unblemished years on the police force, and a strong religious background.

"It is depressing to endure such punishment," Bartlett was quoted as saying in one of the papers. "But Joshua said be strong and of good courage and be not afraid. I keep thinking of those words."

I have to concede right away that our ballistics evidence, though it got Bartlett indicted, wasn't worth much. Williams pointed out that "wadcutters" can be purchased in any gun and ammunition store. You don't have to be a policeman to have them. And that's true.

Secondly, when I sent the bullets and Bartlett's revolver to the FBI lab, to double-check our local ballistics man, the FBI said that though our ballistics man was right in noting the similar markings on the bullets and gun, it was not enough to be conclusive that the fatal bullets were fired from that gun.

Everything about that gun business was bad news. I decided to try to familiarize myself with the weapon involved, so I went to the ballistics lab and asked if I could fire a .38. I held it about a foot away from the shooting box, a box stuffed with padding that stops the bullet.

I guess when I pulled the trigger I jerked my arm . . . because when I looked around after firing, every cop in the place was on the floor. The bullet missed the box, went out the window, and lodged in the roof of the Lutheran church across the street. Nobody was hurt. (The police chief later sent me a little note asking if I planned to pay for the window. I sent the note to the district attorney, claiming it was all in the line of duty.)

Anyway, while Harry Bartlett was making the papers quoting the Bible, I was making the papers shooting up a church.

I needed to do a little better than that.

I got an idea when I was reviewing the detectives' reports, written just after the murder. The detectives had questioned an elderly couple named Alexander who lived across the street from the bar. They would have questioned everybody in the neighborhood, of course. "Did you hear anything? Did you see anything?"

And Mrs. Alexander had commented, "I wouldn't want to get involved in anything like that." Not "I don't know anything" or "We were sleeping" but "*I wouldn't want to get involved.*"

I quickly read further. The Alexanders had admitted hearing shots, admitted going to the window.

Hadn't seen anything or didn't want to be involved. Which was it? I asked the Alexanders to come talk to me in the DA's office. I put the question to them. And Mr. Alexander said he was afraid.

"I saw Harry Bartlett shoot him," Alexander said.

He knew it was Bartlett because he knew him from the neighborhood. He said he saw Bartlett pumping shots into Manning, heard him saying, "You motherfucker, if you get up, I'll shoot you again." Manning did try to get up and Bartlett did shoot him again. Then, still watching from the window, the Alexanders said they saw Bartlett talking to other policemen. They couldn't understand that. That scared them. If they told what they saw, maybe the police would hurt them rather than protect them.

"The rest of the police force is not in league with Bartlett," I assured the Alexanders. "The rest of the police force does not want a killer cop soiling its reputation."

The Alexanders finally agreed to testify. Mr. Alexander confided he was facing major surgery and felt he might not survive it. He thought, he said grimly, he might not be risking much anyway.

We went to trial with the Alexanders as our star witnesses. We also found a janitor who'd been in the bar and saw Bartlett and Manning talking together, saw Manning pull out his wad of bills in Bartlett's presence, and saw Bartlett and Manning leave the bar together. There were some other witnesses who could place Bartlett in the bar too.

Bartlett took the stand in his own defense and I have to admit he really came across as a sincere man. He said he had nothing to do with the shooting. He was in that bar, in fact, only to check out a report that stolen goods were passing through the place. When I asked him, on cross-examination, why he didn't pass this kind of report on to his superiors, he said he wanted to tie it down before passing it along.

Then Williams, the defense attorney, earned his pay by attacking my star witnesses, the Alexanders. He made quite a lot out of the fact that they had not come forward at the time of the killing. How could they be sure what they had seen thirteen months after the fact if they didn't seem so sure thirteen minutes or hours after the fact?

And the judge, as he is required to do, told the jurors in his charge to them that if a witness makes a positive statement about something that formerly he equivocated about, then the jury must give that statement close scrutiny indeed.

The jury was out two days. I remember seeing some crumpled sheets of paper in a wastebasket in the jury room after they had delivered their verdict that the vote had once been seven to five. I don't know which figure was for conviction and which for acquittal. I don't doubt that the jury had mixed feelings about Harry Bartlett. Usually when a jury acquits, it looks relaxed. They have decided a man is innocent . . . they are happy for him . . . they look at him and smile. But not this jury. They came in looking so grim, refusing to meet Bartlett's eye, that I was sure I'd gotten a conviction.

Maybe what the jury felt was: we think he's guilty but the DA didn't prove it. Whatever they felt, they acquitted him.

Though declared innocent of the charge, Bartlett was not reinstated on the police force. While investigating him, we turned up the fact that he moonlighted as a cabdriver without the necessary authorization from the police department, that he got free drinks at that bar, that he had at least had wadcutters in his gun on the street—all of which are against police regulations. The police didn't have to take him back no matter what the jury said, and they didn't.

Now just because the man was innocent in the eyes of the law didn't necessarily make him innocent in the eyes of the DA. As far as I was concerned, Williams had done a beautiful job and Bartlett had merely "gotten away with it."

And that, quite frankly, is how the DAs feel when I win one from them now. They don't join my client in a toast to his deliverance from injustice; they don't glory that the jury has seen clearly what they, in their zeal, have overlooked. They say, "The son-of-a-bitch got away with it."

And if they take a drink after the trial, it is not a matter of celebrating joys but of drowning sorrows.

15

Bungling Burglars

In my short career in the district attorney's office I was a
real law-and-order prosecutor. I really wanted to go after
the crooks. I really wanted to protect the public.

And I think I hit the high point of that career in the
Lackman case.

William Lackman was a police officer killed when he
interrupted a robbery in process. In the aftermath of his
death, one burglar was killed, four men were convicted
of the policeman's murder, two witnesses died mys-
teriously, and a burglary ring of enormous proportions
was uncovered.

The burglars were known loosely as the K and A gang.
The letters stood for a business intersection in a white
working-class area of the city—Kensington and Allegheny
avenues—an intersection where the elevated trains rumbled by all day and the tough kids from the neighborhood rumbled at night. The name was a nostalgic relic
for these burglars. Most of them, or their families before

them, had moved from that old neighborhood; only the tough image remained.

If the Lackman case was the high point of my prosecution career, it was also the low point. And before it was finished—because of the way it was finished—I quit the DA's office, crossed the street both figuratively and literally, and set up shop for the defense.

It started innocently enough with an afternoon bridge party.

Dr. Frank Washick, a sixty-six-year-old surgeon, and his wife, Anna, sixty-two, had invited members of a local bridge club to play at their home. It was a beautiful home, a small estate really, with sizable grounds and well-kept shrubs and trees.

During the card playing, one of the guests mentioned he had a coin collection. Washick was interested. "I collect coins, too," he said. "Would you like to see what I have?" He was delighted to show off his prizes to a fellow enthusiast.

And when the guest went home that night, he described the doctor's coin collection to his wife. "I'll bet it's worth $50,000 if it's worth a dime," he said.

It was a perfectly natural comment and no harm was meant by it. However, the remark was overheard by the couple's son, who repeated it to a friend, who just happened to be a burglar. And the burglar passed the word along to his K and A colleagues (it's a rare burglar who operates on his own). The mark was too good to miss. An isolated house with $50,000 worth of easy-to-dispose-of coins. That kind of house would probably contain jewelry and bonds, too. Maybe even cash.

There was only one problem. The burglars cased the house and noticed that Mrs. Washick rarely left it—the

Washicks had a twenty-six-year-old handicapped daughter who was looked after by her mother. The burglars would have preferred to enter an empty house, but if the job had to be a walk-in, so be it. A walk-in means the house will be occupied and a walk-in job requires a hit man— a guy who handles a gun and is not afraid to use it.

John Sealy, a thirty-one-year-old tough who was then out on $15,000 bail for the killing of a policeman, was selected to be the hit man. Ordinarily one does not get out on bail upon killing a policeman, but this policeman had allegedly been found in bed with Sealy's wife.

Sealy got his wife's brother, William McIntyre, twenty-five, to come along as driver and lookout.

The veteran burglar on the job was Adolph Schwartz, twenty-three, a skinny little guy, about five feet two inches tall, better built to slip in and out of windows than to pull off a strong-armed robbery.

This trio arrived at 4:30 A.M. under cover of darkness. They circled the block a few times, parked their white Buick sedan at the end of the road, and then crept behind a fence near the doctor's house to wait for the doctor to emerge. They whiled away the time with three six-packs of beer.

At 8:45 A.M. Dr. Washick left his house and walked toward his garage. Sealy and Schwartz jumped over the fence and accosted him. "This is a stickup," Sealy said.

"You're kidding," said Washick.

"No, I'm not," said Sealy, and to prove it he waved his gun and pushed the doctor back toward the house. The doctor made an attempt to tackle Sealy on the steps but won only a smash on the head with a revolver butt for his efforts. Inside the house, Mrs. Washick washed her husband's head wound and asked if she could go get her daughter. That was okay with the burglars; they preferred to keep the entire family in the kitchen. En route upstairs to her daughter's bedroom, Mrs. Washick quietly picked up a telephone and whispered her address to the operator.

Police converged on the Washick house. The first the burglars realized it was when they heard a dog barking. Sealy and Mrs. Washick went to a window and saw two policemen walking across the lawn.

One of those policemen was William Lackman, at thirty-four a nine-year veteran of the force. Lackman's wife, Pauline, was then pregnant with their second child. Lackman went into the kitchen and met Sealy. There was an exchange of shots. Lackman fell . . . Sealy ran past him and tried to get away across the lawn.

He didn't get far . . . a hail of police bullets killed him on the spot.

Officer Lackman died an hour later in a hospital. He never regained consciousness.

McIntyre, the driver-lookout, heard the shots and took off for home on foot.

Schwartz, the little guy, was on the second floor when the police arrived. He exchanged shots from the window, and then seemed to disappear. Though the police combed the house, brought in search dogs, and set off tear-gas bombs, he was nowhere to be found. That is, until a homicide detective named Anthony Melfi decided to take one last look before leaving. He pulled open a little closet— a cupboard more than a closet—that appeared to hold only shoe boxes. Melfi looked a little closer and saw a shirt collar behind the shoe boxes. He reached in and pulled out a shaking and shivering Schwartz.

The death of a policeman always hits people hard, harder than almost any other kind of murder. We all know he died because he was protecting the rest of us cowards, because he ventured where we would not want to go. So the flags of the city went to half-mast and the mayor and the police chief issued the kind of statements considered *de rigueur* these days in cases like this: that Officer Lackman's death was clearly a reflection on our judiciary; that the blame could be laid to wrong-headed, wrong-thinking, soft-on-crime judges.

The Lackman investigation by the district attorney's office and police took a more practical outlook: the blame was to be laid on Sealy—who had already received the death penalty at the scene of the crime—on McIntyre and Schwartz, and on any others who had helped plan, finance, or in any other way aid and abet the crime.

All were candidates for the electric chair. All could be convicted of first-degree murder because the death of Officer Lackman had occurred in the course of a felony.

Schwartz was naturally tried first. He'd been caught at the Washicks' with a gun and with plenty of witnesses to identify him. You could not lose a case like that if you spit on the jury; the only question was whether he'd get the death penalty or life.

Schwartz did not take the stand in his own defense but his attorney argued to the jury that he was just a young kid, he'd been taken advantage of by those big, tough guys, Sealy and McIntyre. He'd been coerced into this terrible affair. He'd been ordered to shoot by Sealy. Obviously the jury must have forgotten that Schwartz was still shooting from the second-floor window after Sealy was lying dead on the lawn, because it recommended life.

The next trial up was McIntyre's, and it was at this point that I first got into the case. The McIntyre prosecution was not so easy.

McIntyre confessed to his role in the crime when picked up by the police. He thought that Schwartz must have identified him; how else would the police have known to come get him? He wasn't caught at Washick's. The fact was, McIntyre was only picked up because his name and telephone number were found in Schwartz's pocket. A goddamn lucky fluke—or unlucky, from McIntyre's point of view.

The only evidence I had to work with, then, was that confession, and that wasn't enough to ensure a conviction. When a good defense lawyer gets done with a confession, at least some of the jury are going to believe the police put that information in the defendant's mouth, that he was forced to say it. I wanted more evidence against McIntyre than that confession and I got it.

I got it because the case was reinvestigated from top to bottom. I got it because the police put in long, hard hours of dedicated work. I got it because we had some homicide detectives who knew what the hell they were doing.

The first thing I needed was some corroboration of McIntyre's confession. I had to be sure that even if McIntyre tried to take that statement back (which he did), I could show I had more than his word for what happened.

McIntyre told of being behind the fence at the Washicks' house (we picked up the empty beer cans as evidence); he told of walking all the way to his house, a distance of about six miles. He described the route he'd walked. He said he'd had a gun, but threw it away somewhere along that route.

I went back to the Washicks' and I went over every detail of what happened that morning, minute by minute, movement by movement. And I found out, for the first time, that Mrs. Washick had actually seen McIntyre. When the dog barked and both Sealy and Mrs. Washick looked out of the window, she had not only seen the policemen arriving, she had seen McIntyre standing near the garage.

Was she sure? Had she just seen McIntyre's photo in the paper? Was she just saying what she thought I wanted her to say? I pushed on her. But no, she was sure.

It wasn't a conclusive piece of evidence, but her testimony would help place McIntyre at the crime scene.

The police retraced every step of the route McIntyre said he'd walked and timed it. Just in case McIntyre produced some witnesses who had seen him at home at noon, we could then show he could have been at the Washicks' and gotten back by that time.

The police also looked for that pistol. And they asked if anybody remembered seeing McIntyre in the area that day. The police went door to door with McIntyre's photograph, as only a neighborhood cop can do with people whose houses he checks when they're on vacation, whose kids he helps cross the street. I got fantastic cooperation from the police, needless to say. It was easy to get unlimited assistance in this case because the victim was a cop. There, but for the grace of God, went any one of them, leaving behind *his* widow, *his* orphaned children. I just picked up a telephone and the police went into action.

And, Eureka! They found a witness, Mrs. Florita Magill. Mrs. Magill's home was about a block away from the Washicks'. She was in her kitchen and became alarmed when she heard all the police sirens in the neighborhood.

She looked through the kitchen window and saw a strange man loping across her lawn—about ten feet from her eyes. She remembered his face because she hadn't

looked at him casually. She had looked at him question-
ingly. Who was he? What was going on? Why were all
the police cars around?

When McIntyre was taken to the city's detention center
after his arrest, employees noticed he'd developed a rash
on his hands and legs. The prosecution claimed the rash
came from plants he'd rubbed up against on the Washick
property. The defense said it was caused only by nerves.

The police had taken soil remnants from the shoes and
clothing McIntyre had admitted wearing that day. However, unlike the standard procedure on television, they
never managed to send those soil samples off to the police
lab. The trial was one year and four months after the
murder and I finally sent the stuff away for analysis. It
was merely a gesture, because how could I be sure the
soil samples wouldn't change after sixteen months of
sitting in the police evidence room? I brought the police
chemists to court and sat them at the prosecution table
just to make McIntyre's counsel nervous, but I never
asked them to testify.

(McIntyre's defense attorney was Emmett Fitzpatrick,
who is now the district attorney of Philadelphia. That's
how it goes. I left prosecution for defense; Emmett left
defense for prosecution.)

I brought Pauline Lackman, the officer's widow, to
court to establish the identity of the victim. The defense
was more than willing to stipulate that Lackman indeed
existed and was a policeman, etc., etc., rather than have
the jury see this sympathetic widow on the stand. And I,
of course, wanted her to stretch out the tales of when
she last saw her husband, when she saw him in the hospital, how she was told he was dead, etc., etc.

And when she finished testifying, I asked her to sit in
the courtroom every day, just so the jury could see her. A

police car picked her up in the morning and took her home each night.

It may seem callous to make a widow sit through every grisly bit of testimony, to make her listen over and over to the details of her husband's death, to hear police officers talk about the way the blood spurted out of his body.

But frankly, whichever side I'm on, I always go for the personal touch. I want jurors to know they are dealing with flesh and blood—flesh and blood that is pale and drawn, that is weeping. Whether it's a widow saying, "Give me justice," or a mother saying, "Give me back my son," the jurors know there are others involved besides the defendant and the victim.

Maybe it sounds unfair. You may ask: what do you want to win your case on, sympathy for a family or the facts?

I want to win on everything I've got, as long as it's not illegal, as long as it's not perjured testimony. Both sides do the same thing, and sometimes there's a real competition during a trial as to which side's relatives get the seats closest to the jury.

Anyway, sympathy was not, in fact, all I had to use against McIntyre. The closer we got to the trial, the stronger and stronger the case became. We got a warrant and searched McIntyre's house and found a box of ammunition. We hadn't found the pistol he supposedly had thrown away, so naturally when he took the stand he denied ever having it.

On cross-examination, I asked, "If you didn't have a pistol, how come you had all that ammunition?"

"That ammunition," said McIntyre, "is old stuff. It's been lying on my shelf for years."

That was a lie and I could prove it. Howard Wade, a homicide detective with twenty years' experience, knew just from looking at the ammunition box that it had been purchased within a few months of the arrest. It seems there are markings on ammunition boxes, codes which indicate the date of manufacture. Wade knew the code.

And if Wade's word wasn't enough, I got official permission to fly in an expert from the factory in Chicago where the bullets were made. And it wasn't easy to get that permission. It costs money to fly a witness in, to pay him a witness fee, to put him up in a decent hotel for the night.

The district attorney's office has a budget and they want to know if you really need this: "Are you sure? It's expensive. Haven't you got enough without him?"

I almost didn't get my witness to Philadelphia, and once I got him I almost didn't get him on the stand.

The problem was that McIntyre had mentioned the ammunition while answering a cross-examination question. One of the rules of a trial is that if you bring up an issue during cross-examination, you are bound by the answer you get unless that issue is material to the case. In other words, the issue must have a direct bearing on whether or not the defendant committed the crime, not merely on his credibility as a witness or his character. This rule exists in the interest of expeditious trials. If both sides kept bringing up new issues in cross-examination and bringing in witnesses to, in a sense, rebut the rebuttal and then to rebut the rebuttal of the rebuttal, a trial could go on for years.

Of course, sometimes a defense attorney will advise a client not to mention some particular thing until being cross-examined. That way, the district attorney will be barred from trying to disprove it.

Technically speaking, if a DA is sure a witness is lying

on the stand, he could bring charges later for perjury. As a practical matter, though, you won't find a jury willing to convict somebody for trying to protect himself; it is considered a form of self-defense.

The crucial question for me in the McIntyre trial was whether the judge would decide that the date the ammunition was purchased had a direct bearing on McIntyre's involvement at Washick's or merely on whether he had lied on the stand. Different judges would resolve it different ways. Judge Edmund Spaeth, who was presiding in this case, ruled the matter was material, and my Chicago expert testified. Whew!

I have to admit that the defense attorney, Emmett Fitzpatrick, really rattled me when he challenged my right to present that witness. Frankly, that kind of technical use of the law is over the heads of a lot of attorneys and even some judges. And that wasn't the only way Emmett rattled me. He really pushed hard on his contention that McIntyre's confession was a phony, that McIntyre had been roughed up by the police and forced to sign it. It's easy to imagine that the police were not at their courteous best with a cop-killer, but it was the state's contention that they hadn't laid a glove on him.

However, it seems that when McIntyre was admitted to the detention center he was routinely asked if he had any complaints. And he said, "Yeah, I was punched in the face . . . see this black eye." They took a color photograph of him, a slide.

Fitzpatrick, at the trial, produced the slide and said it would prove his client had been beaten.

"Nonsense," I said. "The defense is trying to make a big thing out of a little mark . . . a scratch . . . that McIntyre probably received while skulking about in the Washicks' shrubbery."

The judge ordered a projector and a big screen—and there was the biggest shiner you ever saw. Was I ever glad I didn't depend on the confession alone for my case!

Fitzpatrick also made a big defense out of all the bullets that flew around once the police arrived. He contended it might well have been a police bullet that killed Lackman. We had technicians at the Washicks' digging out bullets and fragments of bullets from everywhere, the trees, the ground, the kitchen wall. We tried to get each officer to remember where he was when he fired and how many shots he fired. Where possible, we tried to establish by matching grooves, lands, and markings which bullets came from which gun. But in Lackman's case, the bullet had passed right through him. No bullet had been found in his body. Fitzpatrick claimed that if we couldn't prove for sure that it was Sealy's gun that killed Lackman, then we couldn't convict McIntyre of the murder. We could convict him for robbery, maybe, but that was all.

McIntyre took the stand, denied any involvement in anything. He said the only reason Schwartz had his name and phone number in his pocket was because he'd met Schwartz through Sealy, his brother-in-law. But there was nothing more to it.

The jury chose not to believe him, deliberated an hour and a half, and found him guilty with a recommendation of life. Two of the women jurors had tears in their eyes; it turned out they'd wanted the chair.

That took care of the three men who went to steal a gold coin collection early one morning, but it wasn't the end of the Lackman case. As far as I was concerned, it was just the beginning.

I mentioned before that anybody involved in a felony that results in murder is equally guilty of murder—a man who plans the crime, a man who finances it. They don't have to be at the scene. And that brings us to Michael Borschell and William Russell and their involvement in the Lackman case.

First Borschell. You might ask what brought anybody to Borschell: he didn't confess, he wasn't at the Washicks', nobody identified him. How the hell did he even get indicted? I wondered that at the time myself, after I'd been assigned to continue the Lackman prosecution. The scant evidence on Borschell was that the white Buick which had been parked by the three burglars had Borschell's fingerprint on the rear window.

The police traced the car. It had been leased from a rental agency in the name of one Anton B. Erenreich. Erenreich's identification card had been used by his half-brother Donald Oldham. Both Erenreich, twenty-seven, and Oldham, twenty-one, were friends of Michael Borschell.

Oldham admitted to the police that he'd done his friend a favor in return for twenty-five dollars.

That was it. Borschell had indirectly obtained and placed his hand on a car later used by burglars. The district attorney was willing to *nol-pros* the charges against Borschell—after all, we'd gotten those directly involved, gotten them good.

But I wasn't ready to drop it.

I wanted to find out how deeply this Borschell really was involved. I wanted to interview his associates, acquaintances, girlfriends, ex-girlfriends, to see what I could find out. Not that I thought they'd want to talk to me. They would probably be afraid to talk to me, unless I could convince them to be more afraid *not* to talk to me.

I tried to make a deal with both Schwartz and Mc-Intyre—favorable recommendations for parole when the time came—but neither was interested. I had better luck with Oldham and Erenreich. They were afraid their involvement with the car was going to involve them in a murder rap, so they agreed to talk in return for a promise of immunity. I asked them to make up a list of as many people as they knew who knew Borschell.

And one name on that list was William Russell, twenty-seven, then serving three to ten at Graterford Prison on a burglary charge. Oldham said Russell, when he was out, had an apartment in Runnemede, New Jersey, and generally made his living as a fence. He had the reputation of giving fair value for hot goods.

Okay, I went to prison to see what Russell could tell me. What Russell told me was "Get out." He wouldn't even shake my hand.

As I left Graterford, I asked the detectives who were with me to write down the name of anyone who had visited Russell in the entire time he'd been there. We looked up the history of each of those persons and aside from relatives we found one Kit Watson, twenty-six. He wasn't all that hard to find. He was doing three months on some minor charge. We brought him into the DA's office and began talking about this cop-killer—and just like Oldham and Erenreich, he got very nervous about being involved in that kind of charge. He said he would talk to us if we promised not to frame him. We didn't have any plans to frame anybody, so we agreed.

Watson told us he'd met John Sealy and Michael Bor-

schell at a card game in Russell's apartment and Borschell was very excitedly talking about this place where
there was supposed to be a $50,000 coin collection—a
doctor's house. He said he'd met Borschell when both
were in the detention center and Borschell had told him
Oldham was talking to the cops. "We should get rid of
Donald," Watson quoted Borschell as saying. "We ought
to get him a plane ticket or dump him in the river." Our
office arranged to have the cooperative Watson paroled
and we installed him in a center-city hotel with proper
protection.

Oldham admitted pulling twenty-five burglaries with
Borschell. He described Borschell as a windowman—a
lookout. Oldham said Borschell had talked to him about
the Washick job: "I have a nut [a hit man].... He's out
on bail for killing a cop."

One person led to the other. We found red-headed,
twenty-two-year-old "Anna May," who was a former girlfriend of Borschell's. She admitted seeing Borschell with
McIntyre and Sealy. She said Borschell had called her on
the day of the robbery. We found tiny, blonde, twenty-
year-old "Mary," who was Russell's girlfriend. She was in
Russell's apartment with Russell and Borschell while they
waited for a phone call from Sealy saying they had the
coins. Russell was going to fence them for 25 percent of
the profit. She was there when the news came over the
radio that Sealy had been killed, a policeman had been
killed, and the doctor had been injured.

It sounds like we went right from one to the other . . .
like it was easy. But what I describe in a few paragraphs
took weeks, months of work—going back to people you
think are holding out, over and over and over. It involved

a dozen detectives from both Philadelphia and New Jersey sifting tips like sand, looking for a grain of a lead.

For example, we found Mary working as a waitress on the night shift in a Kensington restaurant. The detectives took Kit Watson driving every night, going round and round the city, looking for anyone who looked familiar to him, anyone who might know something. And so it was they came upon Mary, and we pulled her in, and she got scared, and she talked.

Mary admitted working with both Russell and Borschell in a burglary scheme. The three of them would drive around looking for houses that appeared empty, with owners away on vacation or just away. Mary would get out of the car, walk up to the door, and ring the bell. If somebody answered, she'd say sweetly, "Oh, I must have the wrong address. I'm looking for the Matthews. Oh, I'm sorry to have bothered you."

And if nobody answered, she would get back in the car. The neighbors would not be alarmed; a young blonde girl ringing a bell would not appear suspicious. The three would then park the car nearby, double back, and burgle the place.

Once Mary had told us this, we knew she had more to tell. When somebody thinks you've got something on them, they'll tell you a lot of small stuff to get you off their back. If this woman was opening her mouth and putting herself in burglaries, we figured it could only mean she really had something bigger to tell.

We intimated as much. Mary told us about one of the burglars' girlfriends who worked as a secretary for an insurance company. When this girl got the forms that people filled in on what was to be insured—jewelry, fur

coats, etc.—she photocopied the information and gave it
to Russell, who assigned it to various burglars: a safe-
cracker here, a walk-in artist there.

We kept turning things up because people didn't want
us to turn them in. We found this jeweler who would sell
very expensive jewelry and then, as a service to his cus-
tomers, he would sell an insurance policy for it.

He would take down all the information: Do you have
a safe? Where do you plan to keep this? Who lives in
your house? As an added fillip, he would (nice guy that
he was) give the customer an appraisal of the item that
was more than its actual worth.

He then fed all the information to burglars who four
months later would go out and pick up the goods. This
thing was so organized that it was a kind of reverse black
market: you could order a $5,000 mink coat today and
pick it up for $2,000 tomorrow. It would be stolen to
order.

And, oh yeah, the people whose jewelry was stolen
would collect more than its value from the insurance company and then come trotting back to that very nice
jeweler to buy some more.

And so we built a case against Borschell.

There was no question of *nol-pros* now. We were ready
for trial. I argued that Borschell was even more responsible for the death of Lackman than those who were at
the house. He'd masterminded the crime—arranged for
the car, lined up the hit men.

Borschell's attorney, Andy Gay, told the jury the commonwealth had nothing at all but a list of Borschell's
friends. So what if he knew everyone involved? That
didn't prove he'd planned the crime.

In Borschell's favor was the fact that he didn't look like a crook. The other guys looked like corner toughs, but not Borschell. He had fine features and wavy hair, and more snappy Edwardian-style suits. He carried himself with dignity. I referred to him as "Baby Face Borschell" to counter that advantage.

Andy Gay was elated when my witness, Anna May, testified that when Borschell had telephoned her he told her he'd had nothing to do with that robbery, he'd only lent Sealy the car. But his elation was short-lived. Mary then testified that while at Russell's apartment she heard Borschell make that phone call to his girlfriend and lie to her.

Gay told the jury that it was all unbelievable testimony . . . all of my witnesses were tainted.

I replied to the jury, "I hope you didn't expect me to bring in rabbis, priests, and ministers. All I could do was to bring in Borschell's associates."

Borschell was convicted—also to life. The jury voted unanimously to convict him on their first ballot. The jury foreman later said he couldn't sleep for weeks afterward, so affected was he by the horror of the case.

And what a shock that verdict was to Borschell. It almost never happens that somebody who was not present at the scene of a crime is convicted of that crime. Borschell, at twenty-five, was facing spending most of his life behind bars.

It was, as I say, a shock. Which is undoubtedly why he offered to help us convict his one-time associate William Russell in exchange for some consideration.

So what we had done to get the goods on Borschell, we now did to get the goods on Russell. We had all the testimony that involved Russell in Borschell's case, and we had even more. We had a burglar named John Kurz, thirty-two, who decided to discuss Russell because "Man, he didn't have anything to do with a murder." And we had another guy named "Milky Joe" (he had an ulcer) Grizzell who was present when Russell was planning the Washick job. If Borschell was our mastermind, Russell was now the mastermind of the mastermind.

He came to his preliminary hearing kicking and screaming and invoking the name of F. Lee Bailey, to whom he'd sent a letter. (I never did hear if F. Lee wrote back.)

I got Borschell a trusty's job in the prison hospital so that nobody would stab him in a fit of pique. Did I really think Russell might be that vindictive? Yes, I did.

Russell was convicted of murder one in February 1971. I was no longer in the district attorney's office then, but I was called to be a prosecution witness at the trial. In June 1974 a statement I had made on the stand in response to a question from Russell's lawyer, was held to be prejudicial by the Pennsylvania Supreme Court and Russell was granted a new trial. I'd said that we had not arrested Russell until "there was no doubt whatsoever that he had masterminded the crime."

At the time, it was not unusual for a district attorney to voice an opinion to the jury on the guilt of the accused, but later that same year such opinions were held to be unconstitutional. I could hardly object to Russell's attorney making use of the new rules of evidence to win his client a new trial since I'm currently doing the same for a client of my own. But the new trial didn't do Russell any good anyway. He was convicted once again.

But there are some loose ends left in this case.

For example, remember good old Anton Erenreich, in whose name the car had been rented? Well, I went looking for Anton when I needed him to testify against Borschell, but I couldn't find him. The reason I couldn't find him was that he'd received a bullet in the brain and his body had been dumped upon a refuse pile in New Jersey. I had been willing to give Erenreich the same kind of police protection I'd given both Oldham and Watson, but I didn't get to him in time. He was found under a mattress by a bulldozer operator.

A bartender named William McBride—he was on parole following a stint in jail for burglary—gave us the names of the two men who had left with Erenreich the last time he was seen. A week after Erenreich's body was found, McBride's body was found. He had collapsed at the bar after drinking a shot of whiskey. Naturally I suspected poison and ordered an autopsy. The medical examiner ruled it was a heart attack. I guess it is possible for a twenty-five-year-old stool pigeon to have a heart attack. Anything is possible.

When I was working on this series of investigations I had the best backup any DA could ask for. The detectives assigned to me were the best. When I was on trial, I had deputy DA Jim Crawford, the best appeals man around, feeding me the law, doing the research on precedents to hand the judges. I never had it so good before—or since.

I was in the mood to clean up the whole city.

Here I had all these cooperative burglars, so why not? One night a dozen detectives and I took Borschell, Watson, Kurz, and Oldham to a Chinese restaurant for dinner. It wasn't just that I was being nice. I wanted to make sure, just in case one of them decided to stop cooperating, that there were others who were not holding back. One of the burglars got a fortune in his cookie that read: "Do not doubt." We all laughed. I assure you there were plenty of doubts at that table. "Am I going to get probation?" "Am I going to get killed?"

Each burglar was taken in a separate car. We toured the city and they pointed out places they'd burgled . . . they'd relate what was taken, what they'd done with it. I'd corroborate what they said with the burglary report in the detective headquarters.

Without fail, the homeowners—including one of our esteemed city councilmen—always reported a much bigger loss to the police, and the insurance company, than what had actually been taken. If the burglars took $3,000 worth, they'd report $30,000 worth was gone.

All thieves do not need burglary tools.

We were on the trail of more than just burglars. The burglars were just small-fry. They can't operate without fences. They can't operate without trucks and warehouses for big heists. They can't operate without businessmen who slip them information. And we were on the trail of the people who were really responsible. Little by little, one link turning on the other, we were getting close to the big guys.

Little by little. "Do you want to cooperate or would you like to go away for ten years?" "Would you like a friendly word when you apply for parole or an unfriendly one?"

We tailed our informants. We found some going out committing burglaries while talking to us. We swooped in and got them with the goods. They got even more cooperative. We had an undercover officer who had infiltrated a burglary group—he'd come across a counterfeiting operation and a white-slavery operation, right here in little old Philadelphia.

And then the investigation was called off. The chief

of homicides in the DA's office wanted me to try some cases. The backlog was piling up again. I raised hell. Not when I'm hitting pay dirt. Not when I'm going to get to people who really count!

In all fairness, there was a backlog and homicide cases are important, but this was important too. Are you just going to mouth off about soft judges when somebody gets killed but not go after the people who really make crime pay? You can pick off a hundred guys like Sealy and Schwartz and McIntyre and it won't make any difference in the crime rate because others will take their places. They are just the hired hands.

I quit.

It wasn't just that I'd been asked to spend my time doing something other than what I wanted to do. That had happened time and time again, and I just did it, with no beefing.

Frankly, I believed that investigation was called off, not to reduce the backlog—I wasn't the only assistant DA in the office who could try homicides—but because I was getting too close to influential people, and that really went against the grain.

Sure, maybe it was just the backlog. Maybe it was just a matter of rank-pulling in the DA's office. Maybe it was —as some speculation had it—that I was getting more than my share of publicity. The fact remains that I would have stayed there—I liked the DA's office—if I hadn't felt that I was part of something that was not quite kosher.

And my baser feelings were not assuaged when, after I left the office, the investigation fell apart. The DA's office didn't even prosecute what I'd put together for them. They called in the burglars and asked if Moldovsky had made deals with them, and then said I hadn't any right to make deals. Nobody asked me. Not one fence was arrested though I had solid cases against six.

I'm sure it didn't help the police morale either. We had all had a taste of the way things could be: effective cooperation between police and prosecutor. The police have the investigatory experience and the manpower and the DA has the power to offer a deal if somebody talks, and together you can learn a lot.

But if all that effectiveness is only used against the small fry, you haven't really accomplished anything.

I'm not the first to quit a district attorney's office and I won't be the last. There are a lot of reasons why experienced prosecutors don't stick around long.

One reason is money. When I left the DA's office I was making $18,500 a year; I made more than that from court appointments alone the first year I became a defense attorney.

But money isn't everything. Job satisfaction means a lot. My philosophy both as a prosecutor and as a defense attorney has always been the same—win. I will try as hard for a client who is charged with smoking pot as for a client who is charged with murder. I will try as hard for one charged with stealing a million as one charged with stealing a hundred. As a prosecutor I wasn't going to waste any tears on the "little guys" who shot a cop, but I couldn't pretend I didn't care about not going after the big guys too. If you are a prosecutor, you have to prosecute everybody involved.

So I decided I couldn't be a prosecutor.

I think in the Lackman case I saw the best of law enforcement, and I also saw the worst.

16

The Quirks of the System

Have I come to any conclusion about justice in my varied years in its service? Sure I have. My conclusion is that justice is an illusion.

I rarely use the words "guilty" or "innocent." I prefer "convicted" or "not convicted" as more accurate. I have found the outcome of a criminal case depends as much on your money, your attorney, and your luck as on your guilt or innocence.

A citizen with money—a lot of money, that is—is less likely to be arrested in the first place. And if arrested, he or she is more likely to have a lawyer—a good lawyer —present at the outset, and less likely to be questioned long hours or intimidated in any way by the police.

With money, you cannot only afford a good lawyer but your lawyer can afford to hire good investigators, expert testimony, and laboratory technicians, who, if they don't prove your innocence, will at least throw up a lot of doubt about your guilt. With money, you can locate witnesses and fly them in from Siberia, if need be. With money you can afford to press for all kinds of pretrial hearings and for a lengthy, lengthy trial. With money, you can at least make the DA miserable.

Obviously, I think money and attorney competence go hand in hand. The man with money hires a good lawyer and knows which lawyer is good. The man with a little bit of money may be able to hire his own attorney but is less likely to know which attorneys are the best. And what's more, the best may be priced beyond his means. And then even the best can't do as much without investigators and all the rest.

The accused who has no money at all can either be better off or worse off than the guy with a little bit of money. That's because the accused who cannot afford to hire an attorney on his own will get an attorney appointed (and paid for) by the court. That means he may either get the best attorney in the city—and all investigations will be paid for by the taxpayers—or the worst attorney in the city and no investigations at all. He may be assigned to the understaffed public defenders office, or to a civil lawyer who has little experience in criminal matters, or to a kid fresh from law school who needs directions to find the courtroom.

One time when I was a DA, I tried to be helpful to a very green defense attorney representing a drunk driver. I told the judge the driver had scored a .12 on a breathing test. The lawyer objected! It happens that at the time .12 was a passing mark.

"I was just repeating the police report," I said.

The judge snapped, "Strike the test from the record." And he found the defendant guilty.

He should have found the defense lawyer guilty.

In the Richard Alston case, I was at first hired privately by the family and was court-appointed when the family ran out of money. There was no requirement that the court appoint me just because I'd already done work for Alston. In this case the court did so; in others, it might not. Legal fees alone in Alston's case came to more than eleven thousand dollars. (My investigator, Wilbur Davis, put in an additional bill.) The total is not as much as some attorneys would charge, but it is still more than a lot of people can afford on their own.

Everything costs money: experts, labs, transportation, transcripts, research. I do just about every bit of work on every case myself. I rely on only two other people— my investigator, and my law partner, Larry Ring, who specializes in civil law but who also backstops for me and gives me invaluable advice. But I do all my own research. I file my petitions in person. I don't want to miss any opportunity to pick up a vibration that might help . . . a comment from a court clerk . . . a footnote in a law journal.

I don't mean to imply that a defendant with money automatically gets off. Experience indicates that's not true.

The DA, after all, has resources too. He has a budget and if he assigns a priority rating to a particular case, he's got a good chance to win it. The DA can have the entire police force at his disposal, plus the district attorney's own detectives, plus the FBI labs, plus the city police labs, plus all kinds of experts, far-flung witnesses, the works.

But it is pretty obvious, I think, that if a defendant with means comes up against a DA who is inexperienced or who is denied the help of detectives or whatever, he's got the advantage. And it is just as obvious who has the advantage when a defendant of no means comes up against the full force of the state.

In criminal cases where the evidence is not always clear-cut, where there are few of the neat endings of TV shows or mystery novels, sometimes an advantage is all you need.

Lawyers try to perfect techniques and strategies which will give them an advantage. Both sides do it. The Criminal Law section of the American Bar Association holds seminars around the country on "tactics which win trials."

At one such seminar, Philadelphia's Dick Sprague, who was special prosecutor in the murders of Joseph Yablonski, the United Mine Workers leader, and his family, explained that he sometimes picks a fight with the judge merely to convince the jury that he and the judge are not in league against the defendant. He particularly does that if the judge has a reputation as a "hanging judge."

He doesn't want the jury to think of the defendant as an underdog.

Barnabas Sears, the Chicago attorney, said he believed in "talking up to the jury (as opposed to talking down), big jury, little you." C. Anthony Firloux, Jr., from Houston, demonstrated the technique he used to help acquit a client of thirty-seven counts of fraud. He said to the jury, "Many lawyers have lost faith in the federal jury system. I don't share that view, because of the sense of fairness I've seen reflected in your faces. I chose you out of the whole panel because I knew you could stand alone . . . stand aloof if necessary."

Thus flattered, the jury obviously gave attorney Firloux their undivided attention.

Some of the techniques employed by both sides are controversial, to put it mildly. Judge-shopping, for example. I've already said that I don't think a defense attorney should accept a fee if he doesn't do it. I know the DA is going to try to do it.

Judge-shopping involves getting to the calendar room, where cases are assigned, early in the morning and pleading, cajoling, and working it out so that your case gets to the "right" judge.

By 9:30 A.M. on an average day in the major trials calendar room, four moderate judges will have cases backed up of defendants willing to waive a jury trial or plead guilty *only before them.* Maybe one trial will get slated before a hard-nosed judge and the attorney in *that* case will be starting to feel "chest pains."

Several other attorneys will be explaining to the calendar judge that they are "tied up" in homicide cases and won't be available for a trial until the following week. They hope that by then the moderate judges will have some open time again.

Judge-shopping is tied in with that other controversial technique, plea-bargaining. Plea-bargaining, of course, is where the defense and the prosecution work out a deal in which the defendant agrees to plead guilty (and thus save the government the cost of a trial) if the prosecution agrees to drop some of the charges, lessen the severity of the charge, agree to a shorter sentence or even to probation, or make some arrangement which will save the defendant from the full impact of the justice system.

A judge is not bound by the bargain made between defense and prosecution, of course, and therefore it is necessary to place the plea before a judge who is most likely to go along.

In October 1973, then Attorney General Elliot Richardson went on national television to ask the public to "understand and support" the plea-bargain agreed to by the Justice Department in the case of former Vice President Spiro Agnew. It is probably safe to say many Americans learned about plea-bargaining for the first time in the Agnew case.

Richardson detailed the government's case against Agnew for extortion and bribery. Agnew was alleged to have accepted thousands of dollars from consulting engineers in Maryland both while he was governor of Maryland and while he was vice president. However, the government agreed to permit Agnew to plead "no contest" to one count of tax evasion (which drew only a sentence of three years' probation and a fine of $10,000) because the vice president had agreed to resign. Thus the government was spared the embarrassment of such a trial and Agnew the possible outcome of such a trial.

There is a lot of latitude in plea-bargaining when the prosecution is willing to dicker. For example, Special Watergate Prosecutor Leon Jaworski agreed to let former U.S. Attorney General Richard Kleindienst plead guilty to a minor charge of which he was assuredly *not* guilty and agreed not to prosecute him on a major charge of which he seemed quite guilty.

Kleindienst pleaded guilty to "refusing to testify" before the Senate Judiciary Committee. For that "crime" he was given a thirty-day suspended sentence and fined $100. However, Kleindienst did not refuse to testify—he *did* testify. He testified that President Nixon had never applied any pressure on him in the ITT antitrust cases. And later he admitted that the president had applied pressure. Had Kleindienst been prosecuted for lying—for perjury —he would have faced the possibility of a jail sentence.

In negotiating a short sentence in return for a guilty

plea, the average district attorney may also consider the office of the defendant, but more likely is considering the merits of the particular case, his workload, his available staff, the backlog, the budget, and the just-plain-aggravation that this case would represent.

The DA may be willing to compromise. Would the victim of the crime be willing to compromise? Maybe not. Does the victim of the crime have anything to say about it?

Usually not.

Of course, it is considered smart for a DA to discuss the disposition of the case with the victim or the victim's family. A DA can explain that he has problems with the case. Maybe the evidence has been suppressed. He can explain that if he doesn't accept this deal, it's possible the culprit will get away completely. The victm may well see it the DA's way. The fact remains that the final decision is not up to the victim. It is up to the DA.

Sometimes an unhappy victim can make things hot for the DA.

When I was in the DA's office, a bread-truck driver was murdered. His wife practically camped out on the DA's doorstep to ensure that no mercy was shown his killers. If the DA's office seemed to weaken (particularly after the confessions in the case were suppressed) the wife ran to the newspapers with her complaints. She even hired a private attorney and threatened to sue the DA's office. She demanded her pound of flesh and she got it.

That's more the exception than the rule.

The person accused of crime who is truly innocent of blame suffers because he can't accept a bargain. If the DA refuses to see the error of his ways, the only way an innocent person can clear his or her name is to demand a trial. And that, of course, means he may have to spend time in jail waiting for the case to come up. The guilty person who has agreed to plead may be out on probation long before the innocent person who demands a trial ever makes it into court.

That means he will spend a lot of money. My fee is the same whether my client is innocent or guilty. And even if he is acquitted of all charges, he won't get that fee back. The commonwealth does not say, "Sorry we bothered you, but here's a refund of the money you spent."

That means he will most likely get the tough judges—the plea-bargainers will have tied up most of the easy ones. And therefore, if an innocent man loses his case, he will get an even longer sentence than the guilty man who agreed to bargain.

Obviously the same holds true with the guilty person who decides to gamble on a trial . . . the roll of the dice is between freedom and a tougher sentence.

One time, when I was in the DA's office, I negotiated a deal for an accused rapist. He denied the crime but his attorney felt he'd have trouble with the defense. We agreed on a sentence of two to ten years in return for a guilty plea. When the accused came to court and heard that sentence, he once again denied the charge and demanded a trial.

Well, if he wanted a trial we were ready to give him one and I was sure I could get a conviction. Then he announced he wanted to plead guilty. This time, he didn't have the benefit of any plea-bargain. And the judge gave him ten to twenty years.

In short, the guy who agrees to a deal does better than a guy who chooses to fight—if convicted. A guy who knows he is guilty can do better than a guy who either is, or claims to be, innocent.

Despite these drawbacks, judge-shopping and plea-bargaining survive because they enable the justice system to survive. If every defendant exercised his right to trial by jury—which he would be likely to do if there were no bargains and all tough judges—the costs of the court system would be astronomical. There would not be enough judges, attorneys, or jurors in the whole country to handle the load. The haggling and bargaining probably produce as much justice as injustice. Who really knows that a longer jail sentence accomplishes much more than a short one anyway? And who would want justice meted out with computer efficiency?

If humans are imperfect, they are also flexible, which is all to the good. I know the law-and-order types criticize the system, but let me tell you, when they get in trouble, they're as quick as the next person to take advantage of every last quirk, of every civil right, of every loophole in the law.

I have found that the public understood and accepted my role as a prosecutor far better than they now understand and accept my role as defense counsel. People ask me how I can defend somebody I know is guilty.

I explain that in an adversary system both sides are entitled to be represented. They are not always impressed.

People accept that system, it seems, only at the corporate level. They are very forgiving of the corporate crook. Yet violent crime is the act of a desperate man. And while I don't hold society wholly responsible, I feel that society owes the desperate man at least the same defense it gives so easily to the millionaire who lies, cheats, runs a company into the ground, and leaves workers without jobs or pensions.

The desperate man has fewer alternatives than the millionaire. I'd ten times rather defend a guy who gets into trouble because of a drug habit or a teamster with eleven kids to support who may lose his driver's license because he was dead drunk at the wheel than any of those Watergate creeps who had both money and power and used it to burgle, wiretap, and harass.

The Sixth Amendment to the Constitution gives every citizen the right to a speedy trial. And common wisdom says, "Justice delayed is justice denied." That isn't the way I see it. The last thing a defense attorney usually wants (there are, of course, exceptions) is a speedy trial. The defense would like a chance to dig up its witnesses and meanwhile to hope the prosecution's witnesses drop dead or disappear.

Naturally, I may yell and scream that my client has been denied a speedy trial, that he was worn down emotionally by having this terrible thing hang over his head for so long. But I have to admit, more often than not the delay has worked to my client's benefit. Delay is the defense's first ally. Oh, there is such a thing as a totally unreasonable delay, but delay by itself is not all bad. And those words "speedy trial" frankly make me nervous.

I think of myself as a basically conservative person. I was tough as a prosecutor. I don't oppose capital punishment. (In fact, as a defense attorney I love it—it enables me to charge higher fees.)

It's just that I don't believe that law and order are best served by maximum sentences for everybody.

It is true that I defend people I don't necessarily approve of. It is true I would starve if I took only innocent clients. And what's more, it is true that getting a good deal for a guilty man is better for my business than getting an acquittal for an innocent one. (The innocent one you never see again; the guilty one has a cousin who is a dope freak and a brother who is a burglar who will bring you their business.) But to get a break for a bad guy can be as much a service to society as getting an acquittal for a good one. It can sometimes turn a bad guy into a good one.

The scales of justice are delicate ones. Keeping them in balance is no easy job.

Besides defending clients, I am active on the Criminal Law Committee of the Bar Association. I try to revise rules or laws I think are unfair to defendants. And, at the same time, I am active in Shomrim, the Jewish law enforcement fraternal organization, which represents the viewpoint of the police. (And my brother Irwin is a policeman.) I'm on the board of the Philadelphia Self-Help Movement, a private organization founded by a probation officer named Joe Ruggiero. The Self-Help Movement helps narcotics addicts, helps them a lot more than jail would do.

I don't think there is just one answer that will solve all our problems . . . and will make our system "perfect." However, my experience indicates that our system will not be *hurt* by giving have-nots a break. Lately, some of my clients have justified their crimes as a matter of defending themselves against the haves. If we can give a have-not the feeling that he has a chance, that he has a good lawyer, that the rules of the game are applied equally, that "justice" is less of an illusion, then that helps balance the scales.

And in the end, it will help preserve law and order. Without justice, there is violence. Whatever we do to equalize justice—to improve the system of justice—improves our chances for a happy and stable future.